COMPLETELY WHOLE

Paulette Harper Johnson
1/13/2012

PRAISE FOR COMPLETELY WHOLE

*"**COMPLETELY WHOLE** is a guided resource, which can easily be applied to people who are looking for full and total restoration. Paulette Harper provides practical principles, Biblical foundation, and personal life experiences to guide the reader along a path that leads to God.*

Understanding the impact of prayer, Paulette includes a prayer at the end of each chapter that will be sure to help the reader establish a connection, not only with the principles in the book, but a spiritual connection with God Himself. Using a simplistic approach, **COMPLETELY WHOLE** is sure to be a resourceful book, which readers can refer to throughout their life's journey."

Cheryl A. Pullins, CPC
Founder, Victorious Living International
Brandon, FL

"Author Harper is to be commended for the useful compilation of thoughtful chapters, application of Scripture, and use of her personal experiences to assist the reader(s) in their quest for spiritual wholeness. Whether you are at a crossroad of your life or seeking to strengthen your walk with Christ, you will find valuable inspiration, encouragement and, most of all, assurance that by choice you can become **COMPLETELY WHOLE**."

Dr. Linda Beed
Author
Seattle, WA

"***COMPLETELY WHOLE*** is a guide one can refer to over and over again during times of need. Ms. Harper's grasp of real life, and her method of dealing with these situations, truly make this guide a learning tool that can be used over and over again."

Tamarra Bryant
Literary Wonders Reviews
Greensboro, NC 27405
www.literarywonders.com

"Wow!!! Without pretense or apology, I believe that Paulette Harper charts a course for anyone who is experiencing the extreme challenges of life's disappointments; (that if the practical principles are applied) it will lead to a life of God's abundance. ***COMPLETELY WHOLE*** is a thoughtful, down-to-earth, yet, Biblical approach to recapture the position of peace and prosperity that God has predestined for every believer. A must-read for all who have the assignment of edifying the hurting."

Pastor Tony E. Johnson, Senior Pastor, Word of Faith Worship Center
Bradenton, FL

"***COMPLETELY WHOLE*** was written with a hint of personal experience, meant to create a lasting touch on the hearts of those who read the pages. As I read through the book, I got the sense that Ms. Harper wanted everyone to know that there is a process to becoming whole, and there should be a desire to becoming ***COMPLETELY WHOLE***.

Never in time as such as we live will the need arise for us to check in with ourselves, and see what level of authenticity we are operating from. Ms. Harper weaves these types of questions and answers throughout the entire book, giving you a way to see yourself as you are, and to appreciate the desire to do something different.

It is a great read, and its truths will follow for days and months to come. As it is Ms. Harper's desire for you to reach your place of wholeness, I, too, say that wholeness is a great place for change to begin."

Dr. Lakita Long
Speaker, Author
Brentwood, CA

"Rev. Paulette Harper is an anointed author and is led by God as she pens this thought-provoking inspirational book. A must-read, it is inspiring, and speaks growth to our souls."

Donna Moses, President
Sistahs in Conversation &
Sistahs in Harmony Christian Book Club

"When I signed up to read and review Paulette's new book, I was clueless as to how it would target areas in my life. Pains and heartaches I clung to. But it did. Dead on.

Sometimes we need a picture drawn in order to see what we've allowed to hinder us from a closer relationship with Christ. Paulette's artistic ability at drawing a clear resemblance of "us" is a gift. This book is ideal for a small group women's Bible study class as well as a personal motivational read!

Each chapter, clearly aligning with the passages of Scripture that are included, will bring you to a point of deep reflection of what needs addressing in your heart. Through challenges and changes, Paulette encourages us to embrace what God wants to do in our lives! As Paulette closes each chapter with a prayer, you are invited to carry each need of your life, each problem to Christ--to allow Him full access to address the issues once and for all!

I encourage you to contact Paulette Harper and get a copy of this book for your next women's study group and/or retreat!"

Devotional Writer
http://www.theknightlynews.net
Angie Knight

ALSO BY PAULETTE HARPER

That Was Then, This Is Now: This Broken Vessel Restored

Victorious Living for Women

Scripture quotations from the "MSG" are taken from the Message Bible. Copyright (c) by Eugene H. Peterson 1993, 1994, 1995, 1996, 2000, 2001, 2002. Used by permission of NavPress Publishing Group.

All Scripture quotations unless otherwise indicated, are taken from The Applied Bible, Old Testament, Copyright (c) 1965, 1987, by the Zondervan Corporation. Used by permission. All rights reserved.

All Scripture quotations, unless otherwise indicated, are taken from The Amplified Bible, New Testament. Copyright (c) 1954, 1958, 1987, by The Lockman Foundation. Used by permission.

Scripture quotations marked "NKJV" are taken from the New King James Version. Copyright © 1982 by Thomas Nelson, Inc. Used by permission. All rights reserved.

Scripture quotations marked "KJV" are taken from the Holy Bible, King James Verison, Cambridge, 1769. Used by permission.

Editor: Felecia S. Killings of PFL Publishing
Interior Design: TWA Solutions
www.TWASolutions.com

Cover Design and Images: Tyora Moody / Tywebbin.com

COMPLETELY WHOLE
Copyright©2010
Published by Thy Word Publishing
Richmond, CA 94806
www.pauletteharper.com

Library of Congress Cataloging-in-Publication Data
ISBN 13: 978-0-615-33101-0
ISBN 10: 0-615-33101-7

1. Christian Living 2. Practical life   3. Encouragement 4. Inspirational

No part of this publication may be reproduced, stored in a retrieval system or transmitted in any way by any means, electronic, mechanical, photocopy, recording or otherwise without the prior permission of the author except as provided by USA copyright law.

Printed in the United States of America

ACKNOWLEDGMENTS

"Thank [God] in everything [no matter what the circumstances may be, be thankful and give thanks], for this is the will of God for you [who are] in Christ Jesus [the Revealer and Mediator of that will]"
(1 Thessalonians 5:18 AMP).

This book could not have happened without so many people. First and foremost is my LORD AND SAVIOR, JESUS CHRIST. Thank You for using my gift to be a blessing to others and to use it for Your glory. I am reminded everyday of Your favor and blessings on my life. You continue to open up doors of opportunity for me to share my gift to the world. As I continue to write, may what I pen always be inspired by the Holy Spirit. You continue to do great things for me.

To my husband and the love of my life, Tony E. Johnson: Thank you for your willingness to share me with the world and your remarkable spiritual leadership. But most of all, thank you for your prayers, support and unconditional love.

To my best friends, BeNita, and Leah: Thank you for your words of wisdom and the friendship that has developed over the years.

To Tamara, Elaine, and Cynthia: I still remember the day God spoke prophetically to each of us. God is faithful to fulfill every word and promise that He makes. God brought us together, and that bond remains. I couldn't resist giving a shout-out to you!

To my siblings: Thank you for everything you do to help me reach my God given-destiny.

Finally, to my spiritual family at Word of Faith Worship Center: Thank you for embracing me as your spiritual mother.

COMPLETELY WHOLE

PAULETTE HARPER

Thy Word Publishing

Table of Contents

Acknowledgments

Foreword xvii

Introduction 1

1. Lord, I Am Made Whole By My Experiences 5
2. Lord, You Know What Is Best For Me 18
3. Lord, I Will Not Look Back 30
4. Lord, Make Me Whole: Spirit, Soul and Body 48
5. Lord, Your Forgiveness Makes Me Whole 57
6. Completely Whole By Your Love 67
7. Lord, Your Word Has Made Me Whole 74
8. Lord, Faith In You Has Made Me Whole 87
9. Lord, Still I Rise 98
10. Completely Whole, Celebrating Me 106
11. Completely Whole, Fulfilling Purpose 109
12. Completely Whole, I'm Willing To Endure 124
13. Lord, I Have Not Lacked Anything 147

COMPLETELY WHOLE

Colossians 2:1-10 KJV

"For I would that ye knew what great conflict I have for you, and for them at Laodicea, and for as many as have not seen my face in the flesh;

That their hearts might be comforted, being knit together in love, and unto all riches of the full assurance of understanding, to the acknowledgement of the mystery of God, and of the Father, and of Christ; In whom are hid all the treasures of wisdom and knowledge.

And this I say, lest any man should beguile you with enticing words.

For though I be absent in the flesh, yet am I with you in the spirit, joying and beholding your order, and the steadfastness of your faith in Christ.

As ye have therefore received Christ Jesus the Lord, so walk ye in him:

Rooted and built up in him, and established in the faith, as ye have been taught, abounding therein with thanksgiving. Beware lest any man spoil you through philosophy and vain deceit, after the tradition of men, after the rudiments of the world, and not after Christ.

For in him dwelleth all the fulness of the Godhead bodily. And ye are complete in him, which is the head of all principality and power."

FOREWORD

As expected, Paulette Harper delivers tenacious, life-changing material. *Completely Whole* gives a very practical, every day approach to becoming all Christ has purposed you to be. The book touches on each area of life, and gives the reader a sense of urgency to tap into one's purpose now! By comparing various Biblical characters and scenarios, *Completely Whole* walks you through your past and present, and thrusts you into your Christ-purposed future. At the same time, Harper lets you know that the fight isn't over, but it's all about how you receive, process, and handle specific situations.

Breathing a breath of fresh air into Christian writing, Harper's work is consistent, thought-out, and well-organized. The writing format tempts the reader to flip the pages forward to learn more about what solutions are necessary to apply to today's situation.

Unselfishly, Harper pulls on various resources to validate and add creditability to *Completely Whole*. She gives Biblical Scriptures and dictionary definitions to the reader instead of giving her own opinions. *Completely Whole* surely isn't a one-time read!

> Reverend Jamar R. Suber,
> Complete Vision Ministries, Int, Jacksonville, FL

INTRODUCTION

When I decided to pursue my writing career, I knew of no other author who could guide me through the process. Those I expressed my aspirations with looked at me with disbelief. Although they may not have openly questioned my goals, I knew that in the back of their minds, they questioned my success. It was the kind of skepticism that whispered, "Oh yeah, we've heard that before!" But I never allowed their disbelief to influence the direction I believed God was taking me.

I wasn't sure where I was going or even how to begin such a journey, but one thing I knew for sure was that I believed in God. I had absolute confidence in His character. I knew that if God had put the desire to write within me, He would definitely give me whatever tools necessary to fulfill His will. As the Scriptures read, "Delight yourself in the Lord and He will give you the desires of your heart" (Psalms 37:4 NKJV).

My story is different from other writers. I didn't grow up with the aspiration to become a professional writer. On the contrary, I simply wanted to get married, have children, and do the work of God.

As a child, I didn't know anything about becoming a celebrity. I knew just enough to appreciate that those on TV and radio did something to impact others' lives. I did realize, however, that the common bond shared among celebrities was that they knew how to connect with people. They had something that others wanted, and celebrities knew how to reach the public to meet their (the public's) needs.

When God spoke to my heart about writing, I knew He wanted me to inscribe inspirational books, ones that encouraged, motivated, and inspired readers to partake in a closer walk with Him. It was from this vision that my writing career began.

For every person who questioned my motives with doubt and disbelief, there were people who also encouraged me, gladly welcoming my books and articles with confidence. They were convinced that the same words that inspired them could also inspire others, and as such, they should be shared with the world. Such encouragement continues to guide me as I write for the Lord today. I stand in awe knowing that God, who does not make a mistake (and does all things well), could use me to translate His very thoughts, intents, and purposes to the world.

I count it a blessing and an honor that God would use me to write books that connect women worldwide, and touch women from every walk of life imaginable. Many of these women desire to find their purpose, and many are in desperate need of emotional, physical, and spiritual wholeness. To these women, I say the following: Walk with me on this very personal journey of faith and restoration, which is woven throughout the pages

Introduction

of this book; you will discover a process of becoming *Completely Whole*. While it is not always easy, change and growth are inevitable if you desire to be conformed to the image of Christ. As you read *Completely Whole*, may it serve as a guide to bring you to a place of wholeness in spirit, soul, and body.

At the conclusion of each chapter, you will find a prayer of affirmation, reminding you that God has done a complete work in your lives once and for all.

CHAPTER 1
Lord, I Am Made Whole By My Experiences

Wouldn't life be so much better if we could tell God how to do His job? Or maybe we could assist Him or give Him some advice on how to deal with our issues. Wouldn't we simply make sure we avoided much of the pain, sorrow, and disappointment life brought? The answer is a resounding yes! Avoiding hardship, pain, and heartache would be our primary solution in dealing with everything that life brings our way. If we could just sit back and live in complete harmony and joy, wouldn't that be wonderful? Who wouldn't want this kind of life?

Unfortunately, the world in which we live doesn't allow this type of ease. We call this kind of world imaginary, make-believe, or a fairy tale. Fairy tales are fables created for children with the illusion that the world is an ideal and wonderful place, a place, where there is no care or worry, and a place that is free or exempt from negative external influences. The truth of the matter is the world in which we live can be disappointing and cruel with plenty of let downs. Yet, depending on our attitude, the world can also be a place of limitless successes, great achievements, abundant blessings, and untold happiness. Each day that God blesses us to experience is a day in which some type of lesson is going to be taught. The question is: Are we willing to learn?

Many times we ask God, "Why? Why must we endure the things we do?" By nature, we do not embrace new experiences because most experiences require us to give something of ourselves. The truth is we don't want to give anything without a guarantee of a return. We are not willing to surrender, submit, and give God what He asks for in the midst of our circumstances.

We must remember that when we accepted Jesus Christ as our Lord and Savior, we placed ourselves under His authority, His care, and His direction. Laying down our will and yielding to God's will must come from a heart that has complete trust and confidence in His ability to sustain every situation, and resolve every conflict.

When we face a trying dilemma, our question should be, "What is God trying to say to us and teach us?" In life's experiences, if we learn the lessons that God is attempting to teach and convey to us, we will gain valuable understanding, which makes us comprehend more clearly *what* is happening and *why*.

Oftentimes, we do not like how God picks those experiences for us. There are some experiences in life that I can't go through because God knows my makeup, temperament, and personality; the same with you. Some experiences are more difficult to handle than others; yet God, in His infinite wisdom, knows exactly the kind of experiences each of us can bear.

Chapter 1: Lord, I Am Made Whole By My Experiences

No Easy Way Out

As children of God, we want an easy life without interruptions and difficulties; yet we live in a world where our homes, jobs, families, government, and churches are engulfed in turmoil. We often seek the easy road to circumvent the hurdles. Hurdles hinder our progress; unfortunately, we cannot simply go around them. Whatever you are trying to evade, whatever you are plagued with, remember this: You are not the only person who has petitioned the Lord for deliverance. In the Bible, we see what the apostle Paul wrote as he pleaded for God to set him free from his situation:

> *"And to keep me from being puffed up and too much elated by the exceeding greatness (preeminence) of these revelations, there was given me a thorn (a splinter) in the flesh, a messenger of Satan, to rack and buffet, and harass me, to keep me from being excessively exalted. Three times I called upon the Lord and besought [Him] about this and begged that it might depart from me; but He said to me, My grace (My favor and loving-kindness and mercy) is enough for you [sufficient against any danger and enables you to bear the trouble manfully]; for My strength and power are made perfect (fulfilled and complete) and show themselves most effective in [your] weakness" (II Corinthians 12:7-9 AMP).*

In this passage of Scripture, we learn that Paul suffered with a nagging, tormenting aliment that he called a "thorn." The dictionary defines a thorn as: "Something that causes pain, irritation, and discomfort." It's that annoying, frustrating, and bothersome irritant that always seems to raise its ugly head at the worst possible moment. This "thorn" is a constant, painful reminder that we still reside in the flesh; yet we attempt to live, behave, and conduct our lives by the Spirit. It's that issue that relentlessly wars against our soul. Is the apostle Paul telling us that we will live with and carry some type of thorn or nuisance all the days of our lives? It certainly gives us reason to ponder.

According to the Scriptures, Paul's thorn was given to him to keep him from becoming arrogant, conceited, and prideful because of all the awesome things God was doing in and through him. Paul could have easily developed an egotistical attitude since he was chosen to write most of the New Testament. As we know, God used Paul more than any other individual during his time. He heralds this testimony:

> *"Though for myself I have [at least grounds] to rely on the flesh. If any other man considers that he has or seems to have reason to rely on the flesh and his physical and outward advantages, I have still more! Circumcised when I was eight days old, of the race of Israel, of the tribe of Benjamin, a Hebrew [and the son] of Hebrews; as to the observance of the Law I was of [the party of] the Pharisees, As to my zeal, I was*

Chapter 1: Lord, I Am Made Whole By My Experiences

a persecutor of the church, and by the Law's standard of righteousness (supposed justice, uprightness, and right standing with God) I was proven to be blameless and no fault was found with me" (Philippians 2:4-6 AMP).

Paul petitioned the Lord three times to remove the agonizing thorn, but God refused to honor his request. Could it be that what Paul saw as a weakness was in reality the strength of God being made perfect through his infirmity? God's response to Paul's plea is the same response He conveys to us: His grace is sufficient. Almighty God demonstrates His strength and power in what men describe as weaknesses, flaws, or disadvantages. Our weaknesses and inabilities are canvases that God uses to show His might, power, and strength. You must understand that what God is doing in and through you has nothing to do with you, but it is more so for others. We are only empty vessels that He fills with His Spirit to accomplish supernatural acts, perform miracles, and change the world.

Both Paul and the prophet Jeremiah realized that in spite of the miracles God worked through them, the focus of the praise and glory belonged to God and Him alone. As it is written, "*Let him who boasts and proudly rejoices and glories, boast and proudly rejoice and glory in the Lord*" *(I Corinthians 1:31 AMP)*. The Scriptures also state,

"Thus says the Lord: Let not the wise and skillful person glory and boast in his wisdom and skill; let not the mighty and powerful person glory

and boast in his strength and power; let not the person who is rich [in physical gratification and earthly wealth] glory and boast in his [temporal satisfactions and earthly] riches; But let him who glories glory in this: that he understands and knows Me [personally and practically, directly discerning and recognizing My character], that I am the Lord, Who practices loving-kindness, judgment, and righteousness in the earth, for in these things I delight, says the Lord" (Jeremiah 9:23-24 AMP).

All the tributes these men of faith received belonged only to the One who had called them, appointed them, and ordained them to carry out their assignments. It doesn't matter how skillful, wise, or influential one may be. Accolades mean absolutely nothing compared to the knowledge of Christ.

We must continually deal with recurring events in spite of our praying, fasting, and Bible study. There are reasons, some beyond our comprehension, which God allows thorns to remain. The apostle Paul revealed the purpose of his thorn: It was to keep him humble. Some thorns come to bring awareness of how much we must rely on and trust God. Other thorns have been placed in us as corrective methods to discipline us and to keep us tethered to His will. David proclaimed, *"It is good for me that I have been afflicted, that I might learn Your statues" (Psalms 119:71 AMP).* Psalms 119:67 (AMP)

Chapter 1: Lord, I Am Made Whole By My Experiences

states, *"Before I was afflicted, I went astray, Your word do I keep [hearing, receiving, loving, and obeying it]"*

If God does not allow afflictions or thorns to bother us at times, we might fail to seek Him. In order for us to remain humble and not become arrogant, God knows exactly what He needs to do to keep us from experiencing the repercussions of a haughty spirit. I'm sure David believed that the affliction was a great annoyance and brought much suffering. Later, he realized *why* God afflicted him. Eventually, David humbly admitted that he brought the affliction on himself by his own selfish behavior.

Here, David attempts to offer insight on the cause of his affliction. First, David admits that he went astray. His affliction was divinely designed to get him back on track and on course with God's will and purpose. God will permit painful experiences to get us to align with His will, especially when we clearly lack a sense of focus. This is the primary reason the enemy places distractions in our path. Distractions are designed to derail us, to sidetrack us, and to redirect our attention, ultimately causing us to miss our mark. Distractions can create the illusion of being important issues, but in reality they aren't. They're merely illusions.

A distraction can be anything from a previous issue resurfacing to perhaps an old boyfriend, girlfriend, or business acquaintance fighting to recapture your focus. Have you ever experienced a former acquaintance calling you from out of nowhere? These kinds of distractions can trigger an emotional imbalance, causing you to entertain thoughts that are far from the truth. Distractions will take your focus from what God is doing, thereby causing confusion. The enemy knows that if he can divert your attention away from the Father, he can draw you away, causing you to meditate and ponder on things that only have the *appearance* of reality.

Have you ever been driving, minding your own business when all of a sudden an animal dashes out in front of your vehicle? Immediately, your first response is to avoid hitting the animal by sharply veering away from it, which steers you away from your original course. Unfortunately, we are sometimes unsuccessful in our attempts, and we hit the very thing we tried so desperately to avoid. We kill "something" that didn't belong in our path. This is the same way God expects us to deal with our distractions. We must "kill" them quickly, without hesitation. Recognize the distractions for what they are and eliminate them immediately! As long as you continue pondering on the distractions by giving them your attention, they will remain.

David's affliction drew his attention back to God's statutes. He later spoke of his affliction as a good thing. What a transformation of his attitude! Most of us would not view our afflictions as good. Prior to David's troubles, it appeared that learning about God's statutes was not on his list of priorities. Afflictions, heartaches, and difficulties have an amazing way of highlighting what things matter most in life. When we begin to examine why God allows us to experience those things we consider difficult, we find that when we seek the

Chapter 1: Lord, I Am Made Whole By My Experiences

presence of the Lord, He will begin to show us reasons why things happen the way they do.

God knows what is best for us, and He will use different methods to speak to us-methods we don't understand-to draw our attention from what we are doing and redirect it on Him. Because we can be so consumed with our own accomplishments and pursuing our own desires, we often shut God out. Was this David's mindset? Was he completely lost by planning the direction of his life and not inviting God into his decision-making? When we have gone this far, God must do something very drastic to get us to "come to our senses."

What is your thorn or affliction in life? What causes you the greatest irritation? Is it your ex who has nothing better to do than harass you? Is it someone at work who continues to nag and pester you? Is it your constant picking of the wrong mate time and time again? What experiences in your life keep recurring? The very same issues reappear, over and over, day after day, week after week, even year after year. In some cases, the same issues appear in generation after generation. These are uncomfortably familiar patterns and cycles.

"You cry out to God, can I get a reprieve, a little relief somehow, some way?" Could it be that this thorn, this nagging, annoying, persistent thorn is what God is using to draw you into His presence and closer to His heart? Maybe this thorn is really what you need to strengthen your faith; maybe, just maybe, this is what it will take to bring out the best or the Christ-likeness in you.

You may or may not like the situation you are currently in. God understands exactly how you feel and He knows you want out. However, He will *not* abort His ultimate purpose and deliver you prematurely.

God's ways of dealing with us individually are unique. The final results are yet unseen as He guides us on these journeys. He's promised that the outcomes will definitely be greater than the beginnings if we continue to allow Him to carry us to our appointed place. Ecclesiastes 7:8 (KJV) reads, *"Better is the end of a thing than the beginning thereof."*

There are avenues and detours we might take (or make!) as we try to maneuver ourselves out of circumstances; however, trying to find ways out of difficult situations only stifles our growth. We want to get from A to Z without the bumpy roads, flat tires, setbacks, and accidents. But in order for God to get us where we need to be, getting to Z may require pain, hurt, and disappointments. At times, our journey can bring us joy and happiness.

You ask again, "Lord, does it have to be this way?" Again, the answer is yes. God is telling you to learn from every experience, embrace every challenge, conquer every test, and move every mountain by faith. Here is how you must face every challenge: Know that you are already victorious. According to the book of John, victory is won through our faith: *"For whatever is born of God is victorious over the world; and this is the victory that conquers the world, even our faith" (I John 5:4 AMP).*

Chapter 1: Lord, I Am Made Whole By My Experiences

Can you recall the worst times in your life? Can you reflect on how God handled your situations? Would you agree that you would have handled it in an easier and faster way? The answers are probably yes. For reasons beyond our own comprehension, God chooses to deal with us and our problems through long-suffering. Here is how Moses describes God:

"The Lord is long suffering, and of great mercy, forgiving iniquity and transgression, and by no means clearing the guilty, visiting the iniquity of the fathers upon the children unto the third and fourth generation" (Numbers 14:18 KJV).

The dictionary defines long-suffering as "patiently enduring pain or difficulties;" it is the ability to suffer long. Moses is describing the nature and character of God, who is long-suffering and patient. God is tolerant and accommodating with us even though; He knows how long it will take us to choose and live in right-standing with Him. He will sit and wait until we get tired of the way we have chosen to live. God will not over ride our will; rather, He will allow us do what we desire, even though He knows it might kill or destroy us! Selah! Pause, think on that….

Let's look at some characteristics of God's children: lethargic, indecisive, faithless, timid, rude, procrastinating, judgmental, critical, and the list goes on. Despite God knowing how long it will take us to change, He endures our rebellion and disobedience because of His great love for us.

For many of us, God waited patiently while we were intent on destroying ourselves with drugs, alcohol, or other destructive lifestyles. Some of us have been incarcerated because we've violated the laws of the land. We've lived our lives totally contrary to the will and order of God. We have deliberately polluted our bodies by engaging in homosexuality, adultery, fornication and other forms of sexual perversion. We have completely abandoned ourselves to the filthy, lustful desires of our carnal, fleshly nature. Yet our gentle, loving Father God watches, patiently waiting for us to come to ourselves and run into the safety of His outstretched arms. David said this: *"The eyes of the Lord are in every place, beholding the evil and good" (Proverbs 15:3 KJV).*

When we were out partying and enjoying our sin, God was patiently beholding every lewd, disgusting act, listening to every curse word, and watching every foul thing we did. Yet, He waited until we had enough of what this world had to offer, and adopted us into His wonderful family, granting us rights and privileges as sons and daughters of God. If God is willing to put up with us, surely we must be willing to accept the way He chooses to purify us and bring wholeness to our lives.

You might think you are the only one in a state of anticipation, but you are not alone. God the Father is waiting on you to come to Him; waiting on you to realize your need of His guidance; waiting on you to come back home; waiting on you to come to the end of yourself. Friend, are you there? He is waiting for you to acknowledge that it's not your good deeds that are

Chapter 1: Lord, I Am Made Whole By My Experiences

acceptable; it's your heart He requires. Are you still on the throne of your own heart? Is it still all about you? Have you gotten all of your degrees and made all of the money and still find yourself feeling empty? Have you considered God?

Prayer

Father, I come to You in the name of Your only Son Jesus Christ. I understand now the lessons You were trying to teach me. I admit I did not trust You in my situations and circumstances. I accept Your will for my life. I submit my will to Your plan and purpose. When I didn't see You carrying me, You were. I choose to walk in holiness and purity. I want to be made whole through the experiences You have allowed me to go through. Although things might get painful and I might not understand what You are doing, I choose to trust, rely and hope in You. I can't do anything apart from You.

I thank You that through my experiences, I am a better person. Lord, please help me overcome areas in my life that continue to be a problem for me.

Today's confession: I confess today that I choose to walk and live in Your plan for my life. Purify my heart, cleanse my mind, and make me complete in You. I am completely made whole by my experiences.

CHAPTER 2
Lord, You Know What Is Best For Me

My Father's Heart

Luke records the story of a lost son in Chapter 15:11-24 (KJV):

"And he said, A certain man had two sons: And the younger of them said to his father, Father, give me the portion of goods that falleth to me. And he divided unto them his living. And not many days after the younger son gathered all together, and took his journey into a far country, and there wasted his substance with riotous living. And when he had spent all, there arose a mighty famine in that land; and he began to be in want. And he went and joined himself to a citizen of that country; and he sent him into his fields to feed swine. And he would fain have filled his belly with the husks that the swine did eat: and no man gave unto him. And when he came to

Chapter 2: Lord, You Knonw What Is Best For Me

himself, he said, How many hired servants of my father's have bread enough and to spare, and I perish with hunger!

I will arise and go to my father, and will say unto him, Father, I have sinned against heaven, and before thee, and am no more worthy to be called thy son; make me as one of thy hired servants. And he arose, and came to his father. But when he was yet a great way off, his father saw him, and had compassion, and ran, and fell on his neck, and kissed him. And the son said unto him, Father, I have sinned against heaven, and in thy sight, and am no more worthy to be called thy son.

But the father said to his servants, bring forth the best robe, and put it on him; and put a ring on his hand, and shoes on his feet: and bring hither the fatted calf, and kill it; and let us eat, and be merry: For this my son was dead, and is alive again; he was lost, and is found. And they began to be merry."

Can you identify with this lost son? In this parable, the father does not deny the son his inheritance. He gives it to him without hesitation. It doesn't take long for the son to realize that what he had before he left was pretty good. Lack, famine, uncertainty, and fear now had a death grip on him; yet he was a son who had formerly known only abundance.

At one time, this privileged young man, who enjoyed a comfortable life, soon found himself both feeding swine and devouring their slop. The exciting aspect of this story is that the son eventually came back home and the father enthusiastically welcomed him, with open arms. He soon realized that he was better off in his father's house.

God will allow you to make a complete mess of your life, hoping that one day you will realize that in the Father's house is the only place to find complete happiness, joy, and contentment. The Father's house is where you belong, and where all of your needs will be met. It is in the Father's house, you will find rest; and you will be surrounded by His unconditional, unquenchable, and unfailing love.

The father was overjoyed when he saw his beloved son coming home. He immediately restored his son back to his original status, just as though he had never left! What a wonderful father! The doors are also open to my Father's house. Will you come and be my Father's guest?

There is an important lesson we must learn from this passage. The father could have tried to persuade his son from leaving, knowing that the son was uneducated and ill-trained; but there was a lesson that needed to be learned. A life that was once in order and in fellowship with his father was ravaged by his disorderly, unruly, and uncontrolled lifestyle. When all the fun, money, and sex evaporated, he realized that his current residence was not where he was destined to remain. Moreover, it was not the place that his loving father designed for him to live.

Chapter 2: Lord, You Knonw What Is Best For Me

Our Heavenly Father will not force us to walk with Him. He will allow us to experience tough times in life in order to teach us something. The painful lessons we learn result from the experiences we go through and the bad choices we make. God gives us everything in life to enjoy: wealth, free will, jobs, cars, and homes; but it's those things that will force us to realize what matters most in life. The power of choice is something God gives each of us, and our choices will either drive us towards God or lead us further away from Him. Choices have consequences.

The prodigal son never blamed anyone for his current state, although I'm sure those around him exploited him and his lack of experience. There is no doubt that as long as he was generously dishing out the money, those he mistakenly considered as friends were enjoying the conditional pleasure of his company.

How naïve the prodigal son was in thinking that those people really cared about him! Sadly, he soon discovered that those he once dined with, drank with, and made merry with were the first to leave him when his money was gone. His choice cost him dearly. Not only did he squander his inheritance, but he also found himself homeless and friendless. What a price to pay for a bad decision! What a pity to lose everything for a moment of pleasure. Does that sound like someone you know?

Did the son have to endure this ordeal? Yes, he did. This was an extremely bad choice with bad consequences attached. He didn't realize that on the other side of fun and sin was a devastating reality. God teaches us lessons regardless of our willingness to cooperate with the way He operates. Believe it or not, God feels all the pain we feel and knows how difficult our situation is; yet, in everything we go through, we must accept how God chooses to cultivate us as His children. Have you decided to come home, as the prodigal son did? Coming from Isaiah 40:13-14 (MSG), the Bible reads, *"Who could ever have told God what to do or taught him his business? "What expert would he have gone to for advice, what school would he attend to learn justice? What god do you suppose might have taught him what he knows, showed him how things work?"*

Can you grasp that? Who can tell God what to do and how to do it? How can we think God doesn't know what it takes to get us from test to trial, trial to victory, victory to development, and development to promise? Quit fighting the process God has designed. We can't tell God what to do. We can't make any suggestions or vote. He doesn't need man's advice or counsel on *any* matter.

Lord Did You Have To Kill Everybody?

In reading Genesis 18: 20-32 (KJV), we have a story in which God reveals to Abraham His intentions of destroying Sodom and Gomorrah. As the story progresses, Abraham pleads with God five times not to destroy the cities for the sake of the righteous. God concedes, and agrees to spare the cities if He (God) could find at least ten righteous people living in those

Chapter 2: Lord, You Knonw What Is Best For Me

cities. Sadly, the Lord could not find enough people living righteously, and He later destroyed the cities.

We've learned how the man of God interceded on behalf of a people who were awash in sin. Each and every time Abraham pleaded with God, God retracted His plan. God's intentions were to destroy a people whose lives were exceedingly sinful; yet, for the sake of a few righteous, God would have relented.

Can you imagine an entire city living in gross, unbridled sin? Think about this: God could not find any one other than Lot that was living righteously. Abraham couldn't bear to see God do what He had promised, and because God is a just God, He gave everyone time to repent. When there is no repentance, the judgment of God must be carried out.

Our loving Father always leaves a window of opportunity for everyone to reject sin, demonstrate repentance, and turn towards righteousness. We must show Godly sorrow for our actions, especially when our actions and behavior go against the Word of God. God will send someone on our path to share the Word with us, and to help us to see the error of our ways. Yet, it remains up to God to extend His compassion and mercy on people who continue to be rebellious. Once that time of grace has passed, His judgments must be rendered.

In the best interests of everyone, God's sovereign will prevails, even if we as humans (limited in our understanding) naively consider His actions harsh. God has to bring correction to us as His children because He loves us. We may not always agree with how He decides to do something, but we must trust that He knows what is best for us. God's ways of doing things requires our complete trust and obedience.

Did God allow you to experience a tragic loss? Did it cause you to trust Him? Did God allow you to be the victim of downsizing so He could prove that He is Jehovah Jireh? Did God permit an unwanted divorce even though you believed Him for reconciliation? Did you experience His overwhelming, unconditional love when your heart was shattered?

Whatever the case may be, God only has wonderful intentions concerning us. We must always remember that God is omnipotent—He knows all—He sees the "bigger picture." We can only see what is in front of us. As the Scriptures states, *"For now we see through a glass, darkly"* (I Corinthians 13:12 KJV); but God views the entire situation and determines the outcome. As His trusting children, we must understand that our loving God only has our best interest in mind.

Have you realized that the way God does things is best for you, even though it might require you to go through much pain and hardship? Some experiences we go through seem to "hide" our view of God, but don't be dismayed. He'll eventually reveal His plan and design for your life. He may even direct your path through the wilderness.

What is the wilderness? It is more than just a barren place or desert. It is the place where you are going to be tested; or should I say your "flesh" is going to be tested? Here is where your spirit man and your flesh will be at war.

Chapter 2: Lord, You Knonw What Is Best For Me

"Remember our history, friends, and be warned. All our ancestors were led by the providential Cloud and taken miraculously through the Sea. They went through the waters, in a baptism like ours, as Moses led them from enslaving death to salvation life. They all ate and drank identical food and drink, meals provided daily by God. They drank from the Rock, God's fountain for them that stayed with them wherever they were. And the Rock was Christ. But just experiencing God's wonder and grace didn't seem to mean much—most of them were defeated by temptation during the hard times in the desert, and God was not pleased" (I Corinthians 10:1-5 MSG).

To understand the seriousness of faithfulness to God in difficulties, we must look at the effects of our actions while in the wilderness. First, let's define "lusting." To "lust" for someone or something is to desire it strongly, so much so that you are willing to make sacrifices or compromises to get what you want. There are no positive references to "lust" or "lusting" in the Bible. In every instance, it is revealed in a sinful way. We usually associate lust with wantonness and unseemly desire for other people; but lust can also be for things. (Lust for things can also be called greed.) So we see that while in the wilderness, the children of Israel had a strong desire, or lust, to do wrong.

Imagine this scenario. A person has just lost his fortune and is tempted to do anything to regain it. Concocting financial schemes and conjuring up ways to secretly funnel money into his bank account becomes his entire focus. He makes elaborate plans to swindle innocent people out of their hard-earned money. Please remember: In this place of temptation, the enemy of your soul will try to get you to forsake everything right and Godly in order to get you out of your present dilemma. Compromising your morals and convictions will only lead to guilt and pain later.

Let's examine the term "idolaters." Idolaters are people who worship idols or images. Because the children of Israel got frustrated while waiting on Moses to come down from the mountain, they sought out other gods or idols to worship. Consequently, the golden calf was constructed, and the Israelites began worshipping their own idol!

Your patience will be sorely tested in this place called wilderness. Be careful not to lose sight of the Master Potter while here. Temptation will seek to seduce you into looking at other means and resources to replace God. Consider this: You have been asking God to bless you financially. Not just any financial blessing; you've been very specific in your request. Because God answers the prayers of the righteous, He gives you the desires of your heart.

Immediately, you devour the financial blessing and neglect to give God what belongs to Him—a tithe—and you spend the money on yourself by buying material

Chapter 2: Lord, You Knonw What Is Best For Me

things. You are consumed with lust for a new car, a lavish house, fashionable clothing, and exotic vacations. Frivolous, reckless spending becomes your lifestyle. While on top of the world, you feel like you have it all together, and no one can tell you other wise. Wait a minute! Wait just one minute! Did you quickly forget who blessed you? Your worship is not on God anymore, but on your stuff—your perishable, natural, material stuff! Anyone who doesn't have a proper perspective on money will surely lose it. Trust me. I've seen it happen. Can God trust you to do the right thing, and handle the abundance when He gives it to you?

The children of Israel also had a problem with fornication and sexual immorality. I won't assume everyone knows the definition of fornication, so here it is. Fornication is having sex with someone you are not married to. It's plain and simple, easy to understand, yet hard to observe. For single people, this can be a very tough battle. Waiting for God to bring someone special into your life requires discipline and patience, much patience. Please don't be ignorant of the devil's devices; he knows exactly who to send your way that will cause you to fall. The world will tell you it's okay to sleep with someone before marriage or "shack up" (an old term used "back in the day" to describe living together without being married); but God says it's not. The Bible warns us against giving our bodies to those who we are not in a married covenant relationship with. We must learn to take control of our flesh and not allow our flesh to control us.

Preserve yourself for the mate God has for you. I know single people battle loneliness and want companionship. In God's time, He will bring you that special someone. You don't need to shortchange yourself. You are worth so much more than that.

Here is my question to women: Why would any man marry you if you are giving him all the benefits without the ring? My question to men is this: Do you think walking in holiness and self-control is unattainable, or that it only pertains to women? Do you think God gives men a "free pass" to fornicate? The answer is no. Temptation comes to *every* individual; yet, God gives us the power and grace to resist it and live victoriously.

Who would ever think about tempting Christ or complaining? Believe it or not, everybody has done it. No one is exempt from voicing their opinion in the midst of anguish, hostility, and despair. Tell the truth—sometimes, we don't like how God does some things especially when it comes to keeping us in the mishaps, catastrophes, and upheavals of life. We constantly complain, grumble, and nag. We find ourselves disgruntled with anything He does. We become unappreciative of His many blessings. We are always searching; but, never satisfied. Complaining is actually *resisting* God. Complaining implies that He is incapable of leading us through the trial. It is actually accusing God of not knowing how to take care of us. When the children of Israel complained, God wanted to kill them; fortunately, there was always an intercessor to "stand in the gap." Friend, quit complaining! We really don't want God to chasten us as we deserve. Selah.

Prayer

Father, I come to You in the name of Jesus confessing that I have not always agreed with Your way of doing things. I admit that I have murmured and complained in this process You have designed for my life.

Lord, I believe You know how to get me to the place in my destiny so I can grow as a child of God. I submit to You, and the direction You have for my life from this point forward. I choose not to get in the way of the plan You have designed for me.

I realize Your way of teaching me life's lessons will far exceed my own. Teach me how to love, appreciate and cherish every moment in life. I have complete trust in Your Word and promises for me. I will obey Your instructions even when I don't understand where I am going.

I declare that I am made whole by every experience I go through in life. I am free from any impairment, and I lack nothing. I commit my will to Your plan and purpose for my life. I realize I have everything I need to succeed and become the person You ordained me to be.

Before I make any decision in life, I will seek Your face in prayer. I have completely recovered from every experience in life that either came to harm me or caused me not to grow up. Take my life and mold me into the person You will have me to be.

Today's confession: Lord, Your will be done. Lord, do it any way you please. Thank You for bringing wholeness and bringing me to a place of joy.

CHAPTER 3
Lord, I Will Not Look Back

"Do not [earnestly] remember the former things; neither consider the things of old. Behold, I am doing a new thing! Now it springs forth; do you not perceive and know it and will you not give heed to it? I will even make a way in the wilderness and rivers in the desert" (Isaiah 43:18-19 AMP).

Here, the writer, Isaiah, is admonishing us not to give heed to remembering the former things, but to take note of what's happening right now. He admonishes us not to recall, recollect, or commit to memory previous situations and circumstances. Isaiah issues a warning of caution to prevent our minds from drifting away from God's present dealings. He reminds us to refuse to give the previous situations the opportunity to detract us from God's present reality: The new thing God is doing.

As people of God, we often do the opposite of what the Scriptures state. The tendency to rehearse the past is

Chapter 3: Lord, I Will Not Look Back

far too common and far too easy, especially when we have made bad mistakes and bad choices.

Decisions can affect us for years, and with every decision, there are consequences. In making decisions, you are not the only person affected by your choice. Children, family, and friends might also be affected by your decisions. Many decisions we make will alter our future and set the course of our life.

Once a decision has been made, you must carry out that choice even when you realize the effects of that decision. The results of some decisions cannot be erased. Sometimes the decisions we make come out of our emotions, and our emotions can misdirect us; They are not trustworthy. We can be very emotional creatures; and at times, those emotions can be uncontrollable. Where we are right now is due to the fact that a choice was made. Most of us have made some very wise and some very foolish decisions in life.

If you review the course of your life, I'm positive you would have done some things differently. You have probably considered how your life would be different if you had married someone else; what it would have been like if you'd taken that other job; how rich would you be if you'd picked the perfect investment; what if you hadn't had an abortion? Could you have been wiser in choosing your friends? What if you hadn't waited so long to come to Christ? Decisions, regardless of their outcome, were made.

We live with these words: "If only I had known." If we could rewind and undo the last several months or years, we certainly would; but this is not the case.

With all that said, we are all faced with some of the consequences of those decisions. For some of us, we realize that we decided some things in error, error driven by haste. However, it's too late, and the decision has been made. What on earth do we do about it now? Unfortunately, we can't change the past. If you're not in the position of retracting the decision, you must make the critical decision to move forward and deal with the consequences of that poor decision. It's absolutely futile to continue rehearsing "what ifs" over again in our minds. No benefit can ever come from regretting our past.

It's detrimental to live our lives this way because we can never move forward and accept the new stages in life. "What if this? What if that?" We constantly question ourselves. We long to go back and correct things. Our minds drift back in time to yesterday's mistakes. Friends, abandon yesterday's regrets for the sake of tomorrow's glorious victories!

The past only hinders us, and sets a trap for us to fail. We have to kill the past including the statement, "I remember when." Not looking back is a choice we all need to make the moment we decide to do something new. We can never second guess ourselves unless we are absolutely *sure* that we can retract a previous decision.

Does this sound like you? If so, take some advice from the apostle Paul—get rid of that mind set and get out of that pit! He wrote:

> *"Brethren, I count not myself to have apprehended: but this one thing I do, forgetting*

Chapter 3: Lord, I Will Not Look Back

those things which are behind, and reaching forth unto those things which are before, I press toward the mark for the prize of the high calling of God in Christ Jesus" (Philippians 3:13-14 KJV).

Don't you think you have been there long enough? Aren't you tired of the rut? Do you realize that you are wasting precious time in self-pity? If need be, claw and dig your way out of that lowly, unproductive life. How long are you willing to miss out on the pleasures that are ahead of you? There are opportunities that are knocking at your door this very moment.

Are you taking heed to what is being presented? For the sake of our future, we must push onward, hoping and believing that God will take the consequences of those bad decisions and reverse them in our favor. Can you believe Him for that?

Here is God's amazing promise, *"Ah Lord GOD! behold, thou hast made the heaven and the earth by thy great power and stretched out arm, and there is nothing too hard for thee: Then came the word of the LORD unto Jeremiah, saying, Behold, I am the LORD, the God of all flesh: is there any thing too hard for me?" (Jeremiah 32:17, 26-27 KJV).*

Here Is My Story

In my first book, *That Was Then, This is Now,* I was a co-pastor, and married for 23 years before tragically divorcing. During the early years following the divorce, my mind would often race back to the land of "what if" and "if only." What if I had never divorced? I found myself rehearsing and meditating on how things could have turned out differently.

Divorce was a painfully difficult choice. However, once the papers were signed, I had to dust myself off, and push forward, embracing, accepting, and submitting to my new life. Apparently, there was a plan and a purpose that God had for me, which I did not know existed. I had a deep trust and belief that somehow, someway, His original intent for my life would be accomplished.

Divorcing was not the end of a thing, but rather a new beginning. It was a fresh chance for a brand new start; it was a new beginning with new relationships, discoveries, ideas, hopes, and dreams—new journeys with bright new expectations.

Regardless of the changes we have experienced in life, don't ever stop dreaming and believing. Dreams and visions are meant to be shared. If we can see the dream, it has the power to come to pass. It is all in your attitude. David stated, *"For as he thinks in his heart, so is he" (Proverbs 23:7 AMP).*

The mind and the spirit of a person can work for them or against them. The mind of a man and what goes into his heart has a distinct correlation to each another. If what you think gets into your heart, this is what you will believe. What a person thinks about himself and his surroundings will be demonstrated by his behavior. This is a sure sign of what is in his heart.

Chapter 3: Lord, I Will Not Look Back

If you continue thinking on past failures and let downs, it will certainly show in your approach to the uncertainties of life. The thoughts of failures can plague us, even hound us. Because you may have experienced failure in different areas of life, it does not qualify *you* as a failure.

A failure is nothing more than one being unsuccessful in something. In other words, it does not describe or denote who I am as a person. One failure in life does not exclude me from future successes. One hundred failures—or even a million failures—do not alter my God-given destiny! God does not see us as failures, as stupid, or as "less than." He sees us according to the Word of God: as complete. You need to see yourself as complete, whole, and lacking nothing. The Bible says you are:

- Forgiven (Colossians 1:13, 14)
- Saved by grace through faith (Ephesians 2:8)
- Justified (Romans 5:1)
- A new creature (II Corinthians 5:17)
- Delivered from the powers of darkness (Colossians 1:13)
- Led by the Spirit of God (Romans 8:14)
- Above only and not beneath (Deuteronomy 28:13)
- Blessed with all spiritual blessings (Ephesians 1:3)

- Daily overcoming the devil (I John 4:4)

- Strong in the Lord and in the power of His might (Ephesians 4:13)

Starting Over Brand New

"And He who is seated on the throne said, See! I make all things new" (Revelations 21:5 AMP).

Let me share a wonderful love story from the Bible, about two incredible women: Naomi and Ruth. It comes from Ruth, chapter 1:20-21. I love this story because it not only displays total restoration, but also speaks of a woman who was least likely to be part of a ruling dynasty in Israel. Ruth faced overwhelming odds. She was a heathen, a Moabite, and a worshipper of a false god; moreover, she becomes a widow after her husband's untimely death.

Ruth refused to look at her current situation. She adamantly refused to be hindered by what had befallen her. She stubbornly pressed her way through the changes in her life, her disappointments, and the uncertainty that awaited her in Bethlehem.

Naomi, meaning pleasant, journeyed with her husband Elimelech, to Moab for a better life. While in Moab, her husband dies, and ten years later, both her sons die. In spite of the overwhelming odds of surviving, both Naomi and Ruth, pack up what little they had, and set out on their journey back to Bethlehem.

We pick up the story where Naomi instructs Ruth on how to capture the heart of her Kinsman Redeemer, Boaz. There are three distinct things Naomi tells Ruth:

"Then Naomi her mother-in-law said to Ruth, My daughter, shall I not seek rest or a home for you that you may prosper? And now is not Boaz, with whose maidens you were, our relative? See, he is winnowing barley tonight at the threshing floor. Wash and anoint yourself therefore, and put on your best clothes and go down to the threshing floor, but do not make yourself known to the man until he has finished eating and drinking" (Ruth 3:1-3 AMP).

We Must Be Washed

First, Ruth washed. Washing symbolizes cleaning. You must clean yourself of past memories, hurts and disappointments. Our minds must be washed in the Word, and our hearts renewed. Approaching the "new" requires you to be clean upon entering. You cannot enter that which is unfamiliar to you with the same mindset and attitude.

Pray and ask God to cleanse your mind. Are you trying to enter another relationship when you have not cleansed yourself from the previous one? We must allow God to wash us thoroughly from everything that will try to taint and obscure the person we are trying to attract.

Ideally, you want the person to whom you are attracted to recognize that you are well-prepared. Men want women that are clean-clean from head to toe! Men know if a woman is clean. How a woman grooms herself, including her hair, nails and teeth are an important part of creating a lasting impression, and pictures are telling. Drive him crazy, ladies. You have the tools, but remember to keep it holy. Don't hold back. You are a queen, so walk, talk, and present yourself as one. Unclean vessels will only contaminate everything that comes in contact with them.

I Must Be Anointed

Secondly, Naomi instructed Ruth to anoint herself. The anointing represented the fragrances that she would use on her body to attract Boaz. A woman wearing an appropriate fragrance is attractive to the right kind of man. What fragrance have you been wearing? Your fragrance will either allure Boaz or attract Bozo! When you purchase perfume, the oil may smell good in the bottle, but the true scent is not released until it mixes with your unique body chemistry.

Some perfumes smell fine in the bottle, but your nose will be the ultimate judge. Make sure you are sending out the right fragrance message. Your scent should be alluring and inviting. A woman wearing the fragrance of the Holy Spirit—*love, joy, peace, long-suffering, gentleness, goodness, faith, meekness, temperance,* will draw the man that God has for her (*Galatians 5:22-23 KJV*).

There must be something different—something captivating—about your fragrance compared to other women, especially those of the world. When I wear perfume, it not only scents my body, but my clothes as well. When you leave your scent in his presence, he will never forget your encounter. He will remember the distinction between you and other women.

Bottles may look similar, but the contents are not the same for any two fragrances. No two fragrances smell alike. Likewise, whatever is in you will permeate and infuse every place you go. A Godly man who is in tune with the Holy Spirit will continue to seek a Godly woman until his "spiritual nose" detects her scent and leads him to her.

I Must Wear Something New

Throw away those old rags! Did your ex buy that dress, those shoes, or that coat? Throw that stuff away! I've noticed many women have a tendency to wear clothes that express how they feel. When we are feeling miserable, lonely, unhappy, and brow-beaten, we tend to wear old sweats and a ripped-up sweatshirt. Occasionally, I'll even notice a woman sporting an over-sized T-shirt that has been through the wash time and time again. To make it even worse, we walk out of the house wearing that miserable looking outfit. Shame on us! This demonstrates a complete lack of care. It's proof that we have let ourselves go—let ourselves down. We gain weight, neglect our hair, and wonder why no one is attracted to us. I want to make myself perfectly clear: You need to go out and invest in yourself and buy some new, flattering clothes.

A new dress, a new pantsuit, new shoes, or having your hair done will go a long way in enhancing your natural assents…and please don't forget the lingerie.

Did I say lingerie? Yes, I said lingerie. Who said you had to wait for Boaz to look good in bed? You have to upgrade your look and prepare for the man God is going to send your way. There's nothing worse than being unprepared and caught off guard when a muscular, good smelling, Godly man crosses your path, and you're not looking your very best.

Letting such an opportunity slip by can make you feel awful. Remember that first impressions are lasting. This bears repeating: First impressions are lasting! Go get dressed up; the new you wants to come out. Splurge, wash, curl, clip, anoint, smooth, and trim. Put on those new clothes and live in the essence of who you really are. Ladies, the greatest revenge to a broken relationship is bouncing back better, stronger, and prettier than ever.

Let's take some advice from Isaiah 60:1 (AMP). It reads, *"ARISE [from the depression and prostration in which circumstances have kept you—rise to a new life]! Shine (be radiant with the glory of the Lord), for your light has come, and the glory of the Lord has risen upon you."*

The dictionary defines "depression" as, "a low place or low in spirit." Prostration is defined as "utter exhaustion or dejection." Isaiah says there have been circumstances that have contributed to the depression we are going through, and it has caused us to feel overly exhausted and dejected. By the grace of God, we must arise above it all.

Circumstances and situations will always bring out a negative or positive reaction. The wrong reaction from something can affect you physically and emotionally. Life can deal us some devastating blows. Many times, unexpected things occur without any warning; nevertheless, our reactions must be filtered through the Word of God. Place yourself above your circumstances, mount up and ascend to a new life in your mind, body, and spirit.

Many people become sick because they decide to carry the weight of discouragement, failure, disappointment and rejection. David tells us what to do about these issues: *"Cast your burden on the Lord [releasing the weight of it] and He will sustain you; He will never allow the [consistently] righteous to be moved (made to slip, fall, or fail)" (Psalms 55:22 AMP).*

The Bible calls stress, anxiety, worry, and life's pressures loads that we were not created to bear or hold on to. They connect and join themselves with the negative reactions that come from circumstances, creating a toxic, unbearable burden.

The light of God will shine on you. His light comes to bring you out of whatever condition has held you in bondage. His light has the power to deliver and heal. The instant His light shines, darkness must flee—it has no choice. The entrance of God's Word brings light. When God's Word (light) is released, the darkness imprisoning you is dispelled, setting you completely free. The light of

God will shine on whatever has kept you entangled and ensnared.

Friends, rise up out of that pit of discouragement. Your life is not over! Position yourself, and declare that you are taking God at His Word and you are going to break out. Tell yourself, "I'm coming loose." The chains that held me captive must loosen me—loosen my mind, loosen my money, my family, my kids, my spouse, my job, my health, my ministry, and my home.

As long as you have breath to breathe, there is still great hope and promise for a better tomorrow. Capture every moment, and press your way through. Don't allow a moment to pass you by without making a choice to rise above it all. The glory of God is His goodness, and His glory is on you. God is still good, regardless of the circumstances, no matter how severe they may appear at the moment. His goodness will be seen in your life as His grace and His power destroy any bondage that holds you captive. Break forth and shine! You are a carrier of God's glory. Selah.

Decide today that you are coming out—out of depression, out of dejection, out of discouragement, and out of your old way of thinking. There is an open door that God has put before you, and choices to make that will transport you from your current miserable state into a place of God-ordained rest.

Regardless of your current condition, there is a better place that God has for you. God takes great pleasure in seeing you happy. You must decide to move and allow

Chapter 3: Lord, I Will Not Look Back

God to redirect you. Allow Him to lead you to greener pastures and still waters. Allow Him to restore your soul.

There is a wonderful life that God has planned for each of us, and we must take full advantage of all opportunities that He gives us to be happy. Look forward, and plan in advance. Press through, like a locomotive running full speed, crushing everything that blocks its progress.

Do you remember Lot's wife? The angels appeared to Lot and his family before the destruction of Sodom and Gomorrah and instructed them not to look back as they fled the city. Lot's wife (what was she thinking?) did not listen to the warning, and was turned into a pillar of salt. Have you ever wondered what it was that she simply could not leave behind? What was worth her very life? What in that wicked city kept her heart from wanting to move forward? Was it the fact that she too enjoyed the life with the wicked? What battle was she in with her soul that prevented her from wanting a better life with her family? Remember, her fate was determined by her disobedience. Tragically, she died looking back (Genesis 19).

Here we have a family living in the midst of people who did not know God, but rather enjoyed the pleasure of sin. The people of Sodom and Gomorrah were people that lived without restraints, and had no accountability to authority. Ultimately, a day came for God's vengeance.

What will your fate be? Will you die looking back, or will you live looking toward the opportunities that God gives? What are you holding on to that you are willing to lose your life over, and abort any chance you have of progress and happiness?

Are there memories you wish could last forever? Some memories, especially bad ones, need to be flushed out of your mind. Do you find yourself still traveling back and looking through the rear view mirror of life? Are you willing to stay in the mediocrity and the mundane?

If you ever expect to move forward, you must decide to disassociate yourself with everything from the past. You may need to have a bonfire and burn it all— lingerie, pictures, letters, and postcards, everything connected to the past, especially if there were bad memories. The decision is yours. Those items can anchor soul ties. Until you cut the soul ties spiritually, and discard anything associated with the relationship, your heart will never be open to receiving the new things God will bring your way.

All Things New

God is doing a new work in our lives, regardless of the mishaps and misadventures that may have occurred. God is not focused on what happened years ago, even if those things were good. His focus is on the new and exciting things He is presenting to you. The new things God is doing will no doubt drastically improve your life. He is doing something new that has never happened before. What a wonderful approach to living!

The apostle John uses the word "behold" Revelation 21:5. To "behold" something is to gaze at and look upon what is at the forefront of your life. The new thing God

Chapter 3: Lord, I Will Not Look Back

is doing should get attention, and the spotlight should definitely be centered on God. When God does something new, it will absolutely leave people in awe. God is not going to do things the same as before. Can you believe that? Can you perceive that? He is working a work that will astonish, amaze, and surprise not only you but everyone in your life! *"This was the Lord's doing; It is marvelous in our eyes"* (*Psalms 118:23 NKJV*).

Is He calling you into a new ministry that you feel unequipped to fulfill? Is He calling you into a new and deeper relationship with Him? Is He calling you out of the familiar place of safety to a place of faith? Did He give you a God-idea to invent something that will bring you millions of dollars? Are you afraid of starting a new relationship, but you are being nudged by the Holy Spirit to begin again? Is God stirring your spirit to finish that novel, start a business, or expand the one you currently have? What about changing your career? How about deciding to travel places you have only seen in brochures? Whatever the new thing He is doing, rejoice and be exceedingly glad. It's your time, your season, and your turn.

Prayer

Father, I come to You in the name of Jesus. I decide today to put the past behind me. I make a conscious choice to get rid of every memory and picture that I have held on to that reminds me of what I left and those that left me. I cannot change what has happened but I can change how I look at my future. I let go of past failures, disappointments, painful memories, bad relationships, bad decisions, and everything else that has hindered me from progressing.

I choose to live in the right-now moment. I thank You for the new things You are doing in my life, my family, and my ministry. I do not dwell on the past anymore, and I press toward the mark of the upward calling in Christ. I bury the past today, and embrace the new things You have prepared. I welcome the future because my future is bright. I believe You have great things in store for me.

I know the best is yet to come. I choose this day to live in the newness of life. I embrace the new things You are about to bring into my life. I take the memories of the past, and I ask You to remove everything associated with them. You are doing new, marvelous, and amazing things in my life, and I praise You! I refuse to allow my mind to recall the past. I will not go back to that place in my mind that had me in bondage. I embrace and welcome the changes I am experiencing right now.

Today's confession: I will not look back because You have a wonderful future for my life. This is my time, and I choose to enjoy every second, moment, and hour that belongs to me Lord. You know what is best for my life.

CHAPTER 4
Lord, Make Me Whole: Spirit, Soul, and Body

To be completely whole means: (1) total recovery from any mental or emotional hurt, injury, or wound; (2) free of defect or impairment; (3) totally intact in spirit, soul, and body; (4) having all necessary parts and elements; (5) totally absolute; (6) not lacking anything; (7) and able to handle all circumstances and situations with the God-given ability necessary to deal with everything life throws my way. As the Scriptures state, *"Beloved, I pray that you may prosper in every way and [that your body] may keep well even, as [I know] your soul keeps well and prospers" (III John 1: 2 AMP).*

"Prosper" in the Greek is defined as: "To grant a prosperous and expeditious journey, to be successful." The Scripture records that John is praying for the whole man's spirit, soul, and body to prosper and be successful.

God wants us to be whole financially, emotionally, spiritually, and physically. When we are made whole in all areas of our lives, we are victorious, flourishing and doing well in everything—spirit, soul, and body. Every area of my life is prospering, because I line my life up with the Word of God. The spirit of a man is willing to cooperate with the Word, but the soul and body must be brought into subjection.

The soul of a man is made up of the mind, will, and emotions. The mind is the element, or complex elements, in an individual that feels, perceives, and thinks. It includes man's will and reasoning. The will is the mental faculty in which one deliberately chooses a course of action. Emotions are strong feelings, e.g. joy, sorrow, love, fear, and hate.

Your soul has the ability to direct how your mind thinks. Your will directs decision-making, which then affects the direction you take. Your emotions dictate how you allow your feelings to govern. As controlling as it is, God did not create your soul to govern, direct, or dominate your life. The soul is the core of the person that cannot be trusted, relied on, or depended upon. Your emotions will lead you out of the will of God. Being controlled by your emotions comes from the curse of sin, the fallen nature of a man. We cannot be emotionally governed, ruled by people, or even by our soul.

If we allow the soul to direct us and have power over us, we may end up off course. We will find ourselves making mistake after mistake, going from disaster to disaster. Even knowing how the soul operates, we often consent to its lead, direction, and manipulation.

Chapter 4: Lord, Make Me Whole: Spirit, Soul, and Body

When you became born again, your spirit, not your soul, was saved. Your soul must be taught, disciplined, and renewed by the Word of God. For years, past experiences, pain, family background, and education "programmed" your soul. Now we must "re-program" it with Scriptures. Yes, your soul must be taught how to act, behave, and keep in line with the Holy Spirit. At any given moment, the soul will rise up and embarrass you if you do not train, discipline, and bring it under authority. Your soul has been guiding, directing, and ruling your life. It's constantly at war with your spirit for control. You depend on your soul to do your entire decision-making; you gave your soul the ability to direct your thinking; and it became the essential driving force in your life.

Have you ever been somewhere and blurted out an inappropriate comment, and suddenly you realized how stupid you felt? Have you given in to your emotions and lashed out on someone? Have you found yourself crying uncontrollably for no reason at all? Have you gone on binges because of loneliness? Unfortunately, your soul-man has been given a lot of power. However, as you recognize its workings in your life, you must begin to put it in its place. Your soul is an enemy of your spirit.

Although your soul is capable of being out of control, God's design and plan provides you the freedom of choice. God is not a dictator; so He wants you to be able to do as you will, knowing that many times what we pick, select, and decide won't always be to our advantage or best interest.

You should never rely solely on your emotions. Bad choices and decisions come out of our reliance on our emotions. Depending on your emotions can bring disastrous results—financially, spiritually and mentally. The Word of God will bring balance to us as we bring our emotions under the control and authority of the Spirit of God.

A world-class athlete understands that to maximize performance, he must exercise his body and prepare for the day of the competition. If he fails to take the time to prepare himself, it will be significantly harder for him to win the ultimate prize. Serious athletes discipline themselves with hard work. They realize they cannot eat certain foods, and they know they must spend plenty of time in the gym. Discipline and training take time and dedication. An athlete realizes that the results he is striving for will most likely be accomplished because of his intensive training and preparation.

What Went Wrong?

When Adam and Eve sinned in the Garden, their transgression opened the door for sin to enter the world. Complete uncertainty and turmoil now had free reign to hover over the earth and dominate each person. The world was now out of whack; confusion and disorder prevailed (see Genesis chapter 3).

Sadly, the world we call home has fallen so far from God's original plan. In our current culture, children are

Chapter 4: Lord, Make Me Whole: Spirit, Soul, and Body

now being raised by two men or two women, claiming that their illegitimate union and the holy, Biblical union of one man and one woman are equally valid before God and the state. The Bible reads,

> *"For this reason, God gave them over and abandoned them to vile affections and degrading passions. For their women exchanged their natural function for an unnatural and abnormal one. And the men also turned from natural relations with women and were set ablaze (burning out, consumed) with lust for one another-men committing shameful acts with men and suffering in their own bodies and personalities the inevitable consequences and penalty of their wrong-doing and going astray, which was their fitting retribution" (Romans 1:26-27 AMP).*

When the desire for unnatural things consumes the minds of individuals, and they choose to go against God and His Word, God must release them to do what is in their hearts. Because there is a strong passion driving the individual away from God and towards sin, God will allow people to fulfill their desires, even when God knows it's wrong and will ultimately harm them.

Because of these transgressions, we find ourselves engaging in other vices such as stealing, cheating, and even murdering. We have no regard for life. Our youth are now called "killers" as early as ten-years old. We have sexual relationship with more than one person, transferring diseases from one to another. We have orgies and think it's merely fun. I dare not forget "friends with benefits." (Just in case you don't know what that is, it's two people who have the benefits of sexual intimacy, but with no "strings attached".) People who are not married to each other still engage in sexual relations because they are physically attracted to one another. If that is not out of God's ordained order, I don't know what is! *"Claiming to be wise, they became fools [professing to be smart, they made simpletons of themselves]" (Romans 1:22 AMP).* In another passage, it reads, *"Therefore as sin came into the world through one man, and death as the result of sin, so death spread to all men no one being able to stop it or to escape its power because all men sinned"(Romans 5:12 AMP).*

According to this passage, sin entered though one man's disobedience. The result was spiritual and eventually physical death. Every person born is separated spiritually from his Creator, and enters the world a sinner. Sin has become a part of our spiritual DNA. The dictionary defines "sin" as "a transgression of the law of God; a vitiated state of human nature in which the self is estranged from God." The effect of the first transgression is passed from person to person, generation to generation. No person has the ability to escape the power of sin.

Before the fall, Adam and Eve were in complete harmony with God and all of His creation. There were no restraints. Adam had intimate fellowship with his

Chapter 4: Lord, Make Me Whole: Spirit, Soul, and Body

Creator. Nothing was blocking or hindering his ability to come in and go from the Garden until the Tempter came. Adam and Eve were tragically ignorant of the effect their disobedience would have on the world. Because of it, every human born would fall and come under the evil influence of the enemy. All of creation came under a curse and could only be redeemed by Jesus Christ. Sin traveled through the blood line of man, and could only be removed by the perfect, sinless blood of another.

> *"But when the proper time had fully come, God sent His Son, born of a woman, born subject to the regulations of the Law, To purchase the freedom of (to ransom, to redeem, to atone for) those who were subject to the Law, that we might be adopted and have sonship conferred upon us [and be recognized as God's sons" (Galatians 4:4-5 AMP).*

As we read this Scripture, we see that God had another plan to redeem mankind from the power of sin and death. Christ came to purchase our freedom by His own blood. Regardless of the many religions we hear and read about, sin can only be removed by the sacrificial atonement of Christ Jesus, the Son of God. By accepting the atoning work of Christ, those that once were enemies of God are now part of the family of God.

God created everyone, but not everyone is a child of God. The Scriptures reads, *"But as many as received him, to them gave he power to become the sons of God, even to them that believe on his name" (John 1:12KJV).*

Allow me to explain. In order to become one of God's sons, we must accept the atonement and the source of the atonement. Jesus said to Thomas, *"I am the Way and the Truth and the Life; no one comes to the Father except by (through) Me" (John 14:6 AMP).* We must admit that we are in need of salvation, and the gift of salvation comes only from God's chosen Son, Jesus Christ. The Scriptures are crystal clear, without the shedding of innocent blood, there is no remission of sin. Our sins can only be washed away with the blood of a sinless sacrifice. Our good merits alone are not enough to pay the price; they cannot begin to even come close to removing the penalty of sins.

> *"In fact, under the Law almost everything is purified by means of blood, and without the shedding of blood there is neither release from sin and its guilt nor the remission of the due and merited punishment for sins" (Hebrews 9:22 AMP).*

> *"In Him we have redemption (deliverance and salvation) through His blood, the remission (forgiveness) of our offenses (shortcomings and trespasses); in accordance with the riches and the generosity of His gracious favor" (Ephesians 1:7AMP).*

We cannot escape the power of sin on our own for we

Chapter 4: Lord, Make Me Whole: Spirit, Soul, and Body

now live in a world dominated and controlled by outside influences, which are demanding control of our souls. It is essential that we do not allow those influences to dominate us if we want to experience prosperity.

Because of what Christ has done, we can once again align with our Heavenly Father, and be in complete harmony with Him. *"Therefore since we are justified (acquitted, declared righteous, and given a right standing with God) through faith, let us [grasp the fact that we] have [the peace of reconciliation to hold and to enjoy] peace with God through our Lord Jesus Christ (the Messiah, the Anointed One)" (Romans 5:1 AMP).*

When your soul is prospering, every area of your life will also prosper, regardless of what is going on around you. Prosperity is not merely monetary, but it does include that. Prosperity means peace and undisturbed calmness, regardless of the circumstances. It means your business, marriage, and children are successful. It means you are successful, despite what your current condition tells you.

Prayer

Father God, I come in the name of Jesus. First, I confess Jesus as my Lord and Savior. I am a sinner and in need of salvation. I know that You sent Jesus to die for my sins, and I accept the sacrifice He paid for me.

I need to be completely made whole— spirit, soul, and body. I commit my heart to You this day and believe that You will accept me, because I have accepted Your plan of redemption. Forgive me for all my sins and transgressions.

I want to prosper in every area of my life—emotionally, spiritually, financially, and physically. I realize I can't prosper without doing it Your way. I acknowledge my need to have Your power working in my life to transform me and my circumstances. I can't, and I won't, live my life outside of Your divine will. You are the only One that can complete me.

Forgive me for looking to others to do what only You can. You are all that I need, want, and desire. Enable me to grow, advance, and move in every area of my life— spirit, soul, and body for Your glory. This day, I thank You for putting my life in complete harmony with You.

Today's confession: I am made whole— spirit, soul, and body.

CHAPTER 5
Lord, Your Forgiveness Makes Me Whole

The dictionary defines "forgiveness" as "a willingness to pardon; to give up resentment against; to stop being angry with". How can a loving God forgive us of the many transgressions and offenses we have committed, not only to Him, our Creator, but to one another? Forgiveness is the act of one's will; it is the power of choosing. God chooses, and by an act of His will, decides to forgive all those who would accept His goodness, kindness, and mercy. He does it without reluctance and without hesitation. He doesn't give a second thought whether He will forgive you or not. Forgiveness is, however, conditional. What God requires from us is to admit our wrongdoing. Selah. (We'll explore this concept later). *"I acknowledged my sin to You, And my iniquity I have not hidden I said, I will confess my transgressions to the LORD, and you forgave the iniquity of my sin" (Psalms 32:5 NKJV).*

> *"He anxiously awaits and is eager to pardon us.*
> *For You, Lord, are good, and ready to forgive,*

and abundant in mercy to all those who call upon you" (Psalms 86:5 NKJV).

The Message Translation reads, "the pressure is gone, my guilt is dissolved and my sin disappeared". (Psalms 32:3-5). Here we see the consequences of our confessions; it not only relieves the pressure that it has on us, but it has the ability to remove the guilt and eliminate sin.

I don't know about you, but if God would "showcase" (I'm talking about a full color, feature length film!) my sin, my wrong-doing, things I've said wrong, and people I've hurt, it would not be a pretty sight. What about your life story? Would the box office tickets be sold out?

Confessing our wrong puts the responsibility of the error squarely on us. We don't always like to admit when we are wrong because pride can harden our heart. But when we accept that we have transgressed, and we humbly come before a loving God, He will never turn away from us. It's when we refuse to acknowledge and break clean with our sin, that God's hands are tied. He cannot intervene on our behalf.

The forgiveness that God offers is powerful enough to snatch you out of hell. It has the ability to right a wrong, and it removes condemnation, disgrace, humiliation and shame. Forgiveness purifies. His act of forgiving turns His resentment away from you the one who actually deserves punishment, and places it on Jesus Christ the One who paid the price for your forgiveness— past, present, and future.

God will cover your sins and not expose you before people. If you have a humble heart. Exposure of our sins

Chapter 5: Lord, Your Forgiveness Makes Me Whole

comes after our repeated rejection of His mercy. Time after time, He knocks on the door of our heart, beckoning us to repent; yet, we often reject His invitation.

Our natural minds cannot begin to comprehend or fathom the forgiveness of God because we are people, who, by nature, hold grudges and bitterness for long periods of time. It's extremely easy for us to justify how we feel about someone that offended or hurt us, and react because of our wounds, but our Creator is the perfect example of one who teaches us how to forgive.

The apostle Paul wrote:

"Know ye not that the unrighteous shall not inherit the kingdom of God? Be not deceived: neither fornicators, nor idolaters, nor adulterers, nor effeminate, nor abusers of themselves with mankind. Nor thieves, nor covetous, nor drunkards, nor revilers, nor extortioners, shall inherit the kingdom of God. And such were some of you: but ye are washed, but ye are sanctified, but ye are justified in the name of the Lord Jesus, and by the Spirit of our God" (I Corinthians 6:9-11 KJV).

One way or another, we all manage to fall into at least one of these categories. Regardless of your current struggles, the Word of God tells us how God continues to forgive. I'm not exactly sure where you are in this category, but it really doesn't matter. The apostle Paul offers names in which we once were called. These names speak loudly about the character, nature, and makeup of the people we once were. Apart from Christ, we all have lived lives that we are not proud of; nevertheless, Paul points out that we have been washed, sanctified, and justified, not by our own righteousness, but by the righteousness of Jesus Christ. True forgiveness comes from one who has been forgiven of much.

I don't know about you, but I've had plenty of sins of which to be forgiven. During my lifetime, I have offended people with words. I have acted out of my emotions and made decisions that cost me dearly. Yet, everyday I ask God to forgive me. I realize that I cannot approach a forgiving and merciful God without first acknowledging my need of repentance. We must all recognize and acknowledge our sins. And as we face our issues, it is here where God can accept our plea for forgiveness. *"And, behold, a woman in the city, which was a sinner, when she knew that Jesus sat at meat in the Pharisee's house, brought an alabaster box of ointment, And stood at his feet behind him weeping, and began to wash his feet with tears, and did wipe them with the hairs of her head, and kissed his feet, and anointed them with the ointment. Wherefore I say unto thee, Her sins, which are many, are forgiven; for she loved much: but to whom little is forgiven, the same loveth little" (Luke 7:37-38, 47 KJV)*.

Let me point out some interesting things about this lady. First, the Bible describes her as a sinner, one who has not been forgiven, cleansed, or made whole. Regardless of how she saw herself, or how others viewed her, she did not let that deter her from what she determined to present to Jesus.

Chapter 5: Lord, Your Forgiveness Makes Me Whole

No doubt that those who were present talked about her—they were whisperers, naysayers, and haters. They couldn't understand how Jesus could accept this "sinner," let alone accept her gift of costly perfume. How could a holy God permit such a person to come into His presence? Those self-righteous Pharisees had no idea of her degree of pain, hurt, or anguish. Would they know how much guilt she carried from day to day? Would they care about her distresses in life? Were they interested in how religious people talked about her, railed on her, or spoke harshly to her? I'm sure she was not an invited guest; yet, Jesus was so kind, passionate and gentle. He never reminded her of her sins.

She didn't utter a word, but her actions demonstrated how passionately she loved Him. He knew exactly what she needed. He understood the deep, unspoken plea of her bleeding and broken heart. He saw how remorseful she was. He knew what was in her heart. She wept openly before her Savior; she gently washed His feet with her warm tears; and wiped them with her tangled hair. She kissed His feet in grateful adoration and worship. What a humbling, yet liberating experience!

Did He prevent her from continuing? No, He did not. He let her give the only thing she had as an offering of expression of her love for Him. What she came seeking, she received in spite of those who wanted to interrupt her blessing.

What is in your alabaster box? Have you been forgiven of much? Can you show your gratefulness and gratitude in this manner? Can you forgive others as Christ forgave the women with the alabaster box?

When we can see the depths of the consequences of our sins and how God chooses to pardon us and love us, only then can we forgive those who offend us. God made a choice to grant us forgiveness in spite of all the wrong we had done. Once we realize how much God loves us, and how He has provided atonement for our sins, how can we continue in the vain of not granting forgiveness to those that hurt us?

I am made completely whole through His forgiveness, and I am made completely whole when I chose to forgive others. Forgiveness has to be received in order for the power of it to be manifested in our lives. Because the Lord desires an intimate relationship with us, He pardons our sin. Relationships can only operate in the fullest capacity when the people involved walk in divine forgiveness. Even though God has every right to hold us as prisoners to our sins and deliver the punishment that we rightly deserve, His choice is to forgive. *"But God commended his love toward us, in that, while we were yet sinners, Christ died for us" (Romans 5:8 KJV.)*

We have to make the same choice. Although we find ourselves faced with those who offend us, talk about us, and mistreat us, we still must operate and live in forgiveness. When we walk in forgiveness as He has forgiven us, our hands are clean and our hearts are right before Him. *"Who may ascend into the hill of the Lord? Or who may stand in His holy place? He who has clean hands and a pure heart, who has not lifted up his soul to an idol, nor sworn deceitfully" (Psalms 24: 3-4 NKJV).*

Chapter 5: Lord, Your Forgiveness Makes Me Whole

Unforgiveness Breaks Harmony

Unforgiveness disrupts our union with God and with one another. Jesus came to bring us back into fellowship with the Father. This was accomplished on Calvary by God forgiving us through the sacrifice of His Son. God's desire is for us to spend eternity with Him, but only on one condition: that we receive the One who has paid the price. *"And there is salvation in and through no one else, for there is no other name under heaven given among men by and in which we must be saved" (Acts 4:12 AMP).*

Forgiveness cancels our debt—a debt we cannot pay. Without God's forgiveness, we cannot approach His presence, cannot receive and function in the divine will of God, nor can we walk in the full blessings of the Lord. I am connected to God by His act of forgiveness. If God did not forgive us, He could not have fellowship with His very own creation. He created us for fellowship with Him and the family of Christ. *"That which we have seen and heard declare we unto you, that ye also may have fellowship with us: and truly our fellowship is with the Father, and with his Son Jesus Christ" (I John 1:3 KJV).*

The Father's original intent was to always have relationship with His creation. He walked with Adam and Eve–without interruption–until the fall of man interrupted that fellowship. Unforgiveness stifles growth, and blocks any kind of communication we have with each another. It may also delay or cancel any promises He has made to us. In Matthew 6:14-15 (KJV), the author explains how vital it is to walk in forgiveness: *"For if ye forgive men their trespasses, your heavenly Father will also forgive you: But if ye forgive not men their trespasses, neither will your Father forgive your trespasses"*

Here, Matthew points out the conditions necessary to receive forgiveness. We receive forgiveness from God with the stipulation that we forgive one another first. God, in turn, grants forgiveness to those who extend the same grace to others. Did you catch that? Forgiveness from God is conditional; therefore, it's critical to forgive. God knows how unforgiveness will affect our spirit, soul, and body. God is making an agreement with us in the passage of Scripture. He agrees to pardon us when we agree to pardon others.

If God can forgive us of all the iniquitous things we have done to Him, truly we could show more mercy to those who hurt, curse, and mishandle us. I have to make a conscious choice to forgive; and through my obedience to the Word, I can expect and accept His forgiveness in my life.

Forgiving Is My Choice

I realize that some of us may have reasons to hold on to unforgiveness; but in the eyes of God, we must release those that have hurt us. As impossible as it may seem, this includes the rapist that raped you or someone you love, the murderer, the thief, the backbiter, the slanderers—people we feel that are not deserving of forgiveness. We have no right to hold people captive, regardless of what they have done. Remember, we have much to be forgiven of as well.

Chapter 5: Lord, Your Forgiveness Makes Me Whole

I have to make a choice to let God deal with those who caused me injury and trust that they, too, will ask God to forgive them for what they have done. Let people go. Let the sting of the offence be removed. Let the memory of what happened disappear. Don't give unforgiveness any more power in your life. I may not know how deep your pain is, or how you have been scarred, or how much agony you are in because of someone else; but I do know that unforgiveness will cause you to experience physical, emotional, and spiritual problems that could last for years.

Prayer

Father, in the name of Jesus, I come thanking You for making me completely whole by Your forgiveness. I realize that You paid such a high price for my forgiveness. It cost Jesus His very own life. I confess this day and ask You to cleanse me of all unrighteousness.

I acknowledge that if I don't forgive those who hurt me, You will not forgive me. I release everyone who has said something negative about me. I release those on my job who caused me to get fired. I release the one who raped me. I release the person who stole and took things from me. I release my parents for abandoning me. I release my spouse who walked out on me. I release my children who do not respect me. I'm even sorry for blaming You for some of my problems.

Father, I have many sins, but just as You forgave the less deserving, so I, too choose to forgive those who have wronged me. Take the pain away, remove the memory of the action, and cause all the guilt of what happen to disappear. I thank You right now that I am made completely whole by Your forgiveness, and by my forgiving others.

Today's confession: I am made whole by Your forgiveness.

CHAPTER 6
Completely Whole By Your Love

"Love" is defined as "delight, to take delight in, a strong affection for another arising out of kinship or personal ties, unselfish, loyal, and benevolent concern for the good of another". Love is the fatherly concern of God for humankind. Will we ever come to understand or grasp the love of our Heavenly Father? The natural mind cannot comprehend the extent of His love is for mankind. According to the above definition, love arises out of a personal tie or kinship, and kinship connects us with our Heavenly Father by relationship.

When you're in a true relationship with someone, whether it's between husband and wife, kids and parents, boyfriend and girlfriend, or just among friends, that relationship can last through the ups and down, winds and storms—in the good and bad times— if the relationship has a strong foundation.

If I were to ask you what the fundamentals of a good relationship were, what would you say—trust, communication, or faith? Although these are very important elements within the relationship, there is something greater that would hold the relationship intact in the turbulent times. The greatest element that relationships can posses is love. *"And so faith, hope, love abide Faith—conviction and belief respecting man's relation to God and divine things; hope—joyful and confident expectation of eternal salvation; love—true affection for God and man, growing out of God's love for and in us, these three; but the greatest of these is love" (I Corinthians 13:13 AMP).*

We have a tendency to look for love in all the wrong places, wrong people, and in material things. God created us with the need to be wanted and with a desire to give and receive love. Sometimes we get side tracked with the illusion that our desires for and the need for unconditional love will be met by people. There are several types of love that the Bible talks about. Let's take a look at them.

Eros (Greek): This type of love is conditional to situations and circumstances. "Eros" is manifested in the form of sexual love; this type of love is for self-satisfaction.

Phila (Greek): Is where we derive the name Philadelphia, which is the city of brotherly love. This is the love of friendship, best friends, and the fellowship of being with those people you enjoy. This type of love is not reliable because, just like "eros," it can shift based on the testing of times, situations, and circumstances. This type of love expects something in return.

Agape (Greek): Unlike the two previous types of love, agape is not limited by situations or circumstances.

Chapter 6: Completely Whole By Your Love

It is unconditional. "Agape" love is selfless; this is a self-giving type of love. This love is demonstrated by God. God sent His only begotten Son into a sinful, hostile world, knowing that they would kill Him. Yet, without the sacrificial death of Jesus, the world would be eternally doomed. "Agape" love looks out for the welfare of others.

As we see with these types of love, only one of them can be given without conditions. I cannot receive agape love outside of God, for God is agape. I may search time and time again, seeking someone to love me the way God will love me, but it will never happen. This type of love (agape) has to be developed within us by tests, trials, and by the processes God uses to redefine us. God's unconditional love is not based on anything I've done, but it's God's choice to love me without measure. I fall short every day, either by my conduct, speech, or behavior. *"For all have sinned and fall short of the glory of God" (Romans 3:23 NKJV).*

But, because of His agape for me, He doesn't punish me in the way I so deserve. He loves me even when I'm unlovable, uncaring, and selfish. His sheer generosity of pure, unadulterated love, and how He lavishes us with His clemency, compassion, and grace cannot go unnoticed, unspoken, or unrecognized. His incredible love covers us, clothes us, and embraces us even when we're disobedient, rebellious, and "doing our own thing." Yet, He continues to immerse us in His mercy, rapture us in His presence, and fill us with His fervor! No one can do you like God!

> *"But God—so rich is He in His mercy! Because of and in order to satisfy the great and wonderful and intense love with which He loved us, even when we were dead slain by our own shortcomings and trespasses, He made us alive together in fellowship and in union with Christ; He gave us the very life of Christ Himself, the same new life with which He quickened Him, for it is by grace His favor and mercy which you did not deserve that you are saved delivered from judgment and made partakers of Christ's salvation" (Ephesians 2:4-5 AMP).*

His love makes me a complete and whole person. When I consider who I really am, with my issues, short comings, and down falls, I stand amazed. God wraps His big, powerful arms around me, loves me, and corrects me in all my wrong—never, ever withdrawing His unconditional love or acceptance from me...or from anyone. *"For whom the Lord loves He corrects, even as a father corrects the son in whom he delights" (Proverbs 3:12 AMP).*

> *"Sing, O Daughter of Zion; shout, O Israel! Rejoice, be in high spirits and glory with all your heart, O Daughter of Jerusalem in that day. For then it will be that the Lord has taken away the judgments against you; He has cast*

out your enemy. The King of Israel, even the Lord Himself is in the midst of you; and after He has come to you] you shall not experience or fear evil any more. In that day it shall be said to Jerusalem, Fear not, O Zion. Let not your hands sink down or be slow and listless. The Lord your God is in the midst of you, a Mighty One, a Savior Who saves! He will rejoice over you with joy; He will rest in silent satisfaction and in His love He will be silent and make no mention of past sins, or even recall them; He will exult over you with singing" (Zephaniah 3:14-17 AMP).

I herald what Mary said: *"My soul magnifies the Lord, and my spirit has rejoiced in God my Savior" (Luke 1:46-47 AMP)*. There is a huge void in life that can only be filled by the unquenchable love of God. My material possessions can be removed and easily destroyed by fire, wind, and natural disasters. The people in my life can be funny-style, fickle, and unreliable in difficult times.

"My son, reverently fear the Lord and the king, and do not associate with those who are given to change of allegiance, and are revolutionary" (Proverbs 24:21 AMP).

When we look for outside resources to fill the void that only God can fill, our expectations, hopes and aspirations will go unmet. Those resources will only last momentarily, and when unexpected trouble arises, they are the first to evaporate.

Have you ever been in love with someone, and at the beginning of the relationship, you have those goose bumps (warm, fuzzy feelings), and are just plain silly? In the relationship, you thought there wouldn't be any problems, or commotion that couldn't be worked out. But what happened after a few days, months, and even years? For a season, that man or woman filled that void, but when the excitement wore off, you were back to searching and seeking someone or something else to fill that place. And then you were back on the hunt for the next thing that might satisfy that deep hunger to be loved.

I believe this is what happens when people go from one relationship to another. Thinking that the person they are involved with will make them complete, they then realize that the person they are with is just as incomplete as they are. They come to grips with the fact that they are no better off now, than they were days, months, or years ago. Selah!

What must I do then? How can that void be filled? Only by realizing that yearning and searching for love is not in a person or in things can we begin the process necessary to address that deep longing for love. We must come to grips with the fact that becoming a complete person can only be obtained by accepting the "agape" of God. The One who created you knows exactly what you need! Allow Him to complete you and fill your life with what you have been searching for all of these years.

Prayer

Chapter 6: Completely Whole By Your Love

Heavenly Father, I come to You in the mighty name of Jesus. I acknowledge I have searched for Your love from others and in material things, and I have not found what the true meaning of love is. Please forgive me for looking for others to satisfy the longing of my soul.

I accept Your unconditional love that is not based on situations or circumstances, but is only based on Your desire to love. I want You to fill that void in my life and make me a complete person in You.

I recognize that my need of true agape love can only come from You. Thank You for sending Jesus to show me true agape love. Thank You for loving me in my error, and when I go astray. Thank You for loving me back into the sheepfold.

Enable me to live according to Your Word and keep me from falling away from Your unconditional love. I commit my heart to following Your plan and purpose for my life.

Today's confession: I am made whole by His love.

CHAPTER 7
Lord, Your Word Has Made Me Whole

"So shall My word be that goes forth out of My mouth: it shall not return to Me void without producing any effect, useless], but it shall accomplish that which I please and purpose, and it shall prosper in the thing for which I sent it" (Isaiah 55:11 AMP).

Words have the power and ability to create. Words are used to shape and mold our personality and behavior. Our environment and the condition of the world is a manifestation of the words that have been spoken through people. However, you choose to deliver them—whether in written or spoken form—words possess the ability to be effective and creative. Their use determines their effect on your life, circumstances, and on others.

When you release your words, you give them the right to operate and function in the matter in which they have been released. Speak the word in the atmosphere, and see if the atmosphere will change. Once released, the word has the capability to respond, create, and produce exactly what you have told it to do.

There is a right way and wrong way to use words. A person with a negative spirit will not use the power of words to encourage, or build someone up; the opposite effect will occur. Negative people will use their negative words to tear down, harm, and cut those to whom they are speaking. You must consider the spirit and the heart from which the words come from.

> *"A bit in the mouth of a horse controls the whole horse. A small rudder on a huge ship in the hands of a skilled captain sets a course in the face of the strongest winds. A word out of your mouth may seem of no account, but it can accomplish nearly anything—or destroy it!*
>
> *Remember, it only takes a spark, to set off a forest fire. A careless or wrongly placed word from your mouth can do that. By our speech we can ruin the world, turn harmony to chaos, and throw mud on a reputation; send the whole world up in smoke and go up in smoke with it, smoke right from the pit of hell. This is scary. You can tame a tiger, but you can't tame a tongue—it's never been done. The tongue runs wild; it's a wanton killer. With our tongues we bless God; with the same tongues we curse the very men and women he made in His image. Curses and blessings out of the same mouth! My friends, this can't go on.*

> *A spring doesn't gush fresh water one day and brackish the next, does it? Apple trees don't bear strawberries, do they? Raspberry bushes don't bear apples, do they? You're not going to dip into a polluted mud hole and get a cup of clear, cool water, are you"?(James 3:4-10 MSG).*

The book of James says a careless or wrongly placed word out of your mouth can set off sparks everywhere. Have you ever waited patiently for someone to give a speech, or for a minister to bring a dynamic word, but were disappointed because of something they said wrong? I bet you sat in dismay, asking yourself why in the world they said that! And from that point on, no matter how eloquently they spoke, you did not hear another word. What happened? I'll tell you. They did not choose the right words, nor were they conscience of what those words would do to the listening audience.

In your mind, the only thing you would continue hearing are the words they spoke in error. We must select our words carefully. If not, they can make or break our ministry, friendships, and relationships. Have you been in a conversation with someone you thought was brilliant? Yet, you soon found out they lacked proper English and used words in an incorrect manner. I'm sure your perception of them changed. Why? Was it based on the conversation? Most likely it was.

The apostle James says that a tongue cannot be tamed. We are unable to control what we say in our own

Chapter 7: Lord, Your Word Has Made Me Whole

power. It takes our willingness and a surrendered heart to allow the Holy Spirit to help us with our tongue. The power to control our mouth has to be given over to God. Without that, James concludes, our tongue has the power to kill and destroy. "Lord, help me control my mouth" must be our confession. Have you ever said something in a heated conversation and later regretted your words? I surely have. I wished I'd given more consideration to my words. Eventually, I went back to that person and apologized.

You must immediately correct the wrong. Never let someone leave your presence knowing that you owe them an apology. The words you spoke have the power and ability to set the course of life. Tell a person long enough that they are useless, no good, and will amount to nothing, and eventually those toxic words will have a damaging effect on that person's life. It might take years of counseling for that individual to gain the confidence and self-esteem they need to move forward.

The tongue can also be used to control others. A person's own lack of confidence and intimidation can be transferred to others by words. For example, if I have a spirit of intimidation and I'm insecure, I can transfer those feelings to others by threatening them with my words. Do you know someone with control issues? The only way they feel powerful is by speaking words that will destroy another person's spirit. This is definitely not from God and it comes from the pit of hell. The controller is aware of exactly what they are doing and saying. They know how to gain control of someone else by a spirit of manipulation. This type of individual must get help and seek deliverance from the Lord.

Similarly, a person with a condescending attitude uses the same tactics. They tend to belittle others. This is rooted in a spirit of arrogance and pride. These people believe they are superior to others, and they demonstrate it by their actions and words.

God's intentions are for words to bring hope, healing, deliverance, and wholeness to everyone. The nature of God is not to use words to tear down or to destroy. Because He realizes the power and the effectiveness of words, He uses them, knowing they have the creative ability, to bring into existence those things He desires.

"Then God said" is recorded at least nine times in Genesis 1. Something happened every time God spoke: *And God said, "Let there be light and there was light" (Genesis 1:3 KJV)*. "Let" means: to allow or permit. When God spoke and framed the world, He said what He wanted to see. What is it that you are looking to see change in your life? You have the ability and the creative imagination to bring it to pass by your spoken words. If something is out of sync in your life, why not take the Word of God, and begin to form and shape your situation into the reflection of what you want to see based on the Word of God?

God said, and it was so. We can speak whatever we want to see happen in our relationships, homes, ministries, businesses, environments, workplaces, and families. As long as what we speak corresponds with the Word of God, God will make sure that word produces the desired effect. Do you have enough faith to believe that what you say can happen?

Don't Block My Flow

> *"And behold, a woman who had suffered from a flow of blood for twelve years came up behind Him and touched the fringe of His garment; for she kept saying to herself, if I only touch His garment, I shall be restored to health. Jesus turned around and, seeing her, He said, Take courage, daughter! Your faith has made you well. And at once the woman was restored to health" (Matthew 9:20-22 AMP).*

In this passage of Scripture, we learn of a woman with a health condition that profoundly affected her for twelve long years. She sought help from physicians, but found that they could not provide her with a cure. *(Luke 8:43 AMP)* reads, "she had spent all her livelihood on physicians and could not be healed." What is so important in this passage is the fact that she kept saying to herself, "If I only touch His garment." Did you notice that? She kept saying—not once, nor twice, but repeated it. She knew that in order for her healing to take place, she only had to touch the fringe of Jesus' garment.

She kept saying, kept declaring it, over again. She repeated this promise to herself. She had exhausted all avenues of receiving any type of breakthrough with the doctors. But her faith increased when she heard that

Jesus was near. She pushed her way through the crowd, knowing within herself that in order for her to be made whole she needed to touch His garment.

Jesus said, "Whatsoever things you say." He is expecting you to speak to your mountain, issues, situations, and conditions by using the Word of God. Watch God remove those things that have bound you for years, and in the process make you a whole and complete person. Your voice has the ability to create whatsoever you desire.

> *"For assuredly, I say to you, whoever says to this mountain, 'Be removed and be cast into the sea,' and does not doubt in his heart, but believes that those things he says will be done, he will have whatever he says. Therefore I say to you, whatever things you ask when you pray, believe that you receive them, and you will have them" (Mark 11:23-24 NKJV).*

There are times as believers that no one will believe with you. People will think you are crazy—out of your mind—for going against the norm. You may not have anyone speaking into your life or giving you encouraging words, especially during the challenging and pressing times. It is here when you must rely on the Word in you to keep and carry you to victory.

During these moments of intense need, you must talk to yourself, your situation, your finances, and your environment. I cannot imagine dealing with the same

Chapter 7: Lord, Your Word Has Made Me Whole

issues, in the same manner day after day, month after month, and year after year, and expecting to get different results. That's insane! The woman with the issue of blood did something different, something against tradition; she did something out of the box.

She, by Jewish custom, had no right to be in public because of her condition; nor would anyone consider attempting to touch the holy garment of the priest.

> *"And if a woman have an issue of her blood many days out of the time of her separation, or if it run beyond the time of her separation; all the days of the issue of her uncleanness shall be as the days of her separation: she shall be unclean" (Leviticus 15:25 KJV).*

By society's standards and laws, she was impure and tainted. According to Jewish custom, contact with her would have rendered someone ceremonially impure. Thankfully, this woman with the issue of blood knew that all she had to do was touch His garment, and she would be made whole–completely healed–and not lacking anything. The hem of His garment had incredibly significant meaning. It was a reminder of the commandments of God. Additionally, it was noted that Jesus was recognized for having power, authority, and wisdom.

The women with the issue of blood obviously knew just who Jesus was. She knew He came representing God the Father. The Bible describes Him as our Deliverer,

Healer, Counselor, Mighty God, Everlasting Father, Prince of Peace, Wonderful, Fortress, and Sustainer. She may have thought like this: "if I can simply touch the One who possesses the fullness of God–the One who lacks nothing–who, and what He possesses will become who and what I am!" Selah! Wow! If I continue allowing Jesus to touch me, who He is, is what I will eventually become.

She pressed her way through the naysayers, haters, and mockers. At that moment, she was only concerned about receiving something she longed for—and that was to be made whole. She approached Jesus, and knowing where the exact point of contact would be, she broke tradition and received what she had been confessing. If only I could touch the hem of His garment, I would be made whole. Have you exhausted all your options? May I suggest you try Jesus?

His desire is for us to be whole, complete, and not lacking anything. Here is our confirmation.

The 23rd Psalms—(KJV)

The Lord is my Shepherd—That's Relationship!
I shall not want—That's Provision!
He maketh me to lie down in green pastures—That's Rest!
He leadeth me beside the still waters—That's Refreshment!
He restores my soul—That's Therapeutic!
He leadeth me in the paths of

Chapter 7: Lord, Your Word Has Made Me Whole

righteousness—That's Headship!
For His name's sake—That's Purpose!
Yea, though I walk through the valley of the
shadow of death—That's Trials!
I will fear no evil—That's Protection!
For Thou art with me—That's Faithfulness!
Thy rod and Thy staff they comfort me—That's Order!
Thou preparest a table before me in the presence of
mine enemies—That's Expectation!
Thou anointest my head with oil—That's Sanctification!
My cup runneth over—That's Overflow
Surely goodness and mercy shall follow me all the days
of my life—That's Blessing!
And I will dwell in the house of the Lord—That's Safety

Forever—That's Never Ending!

In Hebrew, the word "want" is translated "ehacer" meaning: "lack, fail, to be in want." David had complete confidence in God, and we must posses that same confidence, knowing that God will never leave us lacking. The only way David could make such a great confession is by the relationship he had with God. There were many times in David's life that he faced great opposition and hurdles. Situations would arise in the form of lack or want. But David confessed what he knew to be true.

Numerous times in the Bible, God continued to give evidence of His faithfulness when lack or want appeared.

"For the LORD thy God hath blessed thee in all the works of thy hand: he knoweth thy walking through

this great wilderness: these forty years the LORD thy God hath been with thee; thou hast lacked nothing" (Deuteronomy 2:7KJV).

"A land wherein thou shalt eat bread without scarceness, thou shalt not lack any thing in it; a land whose stones are iron, and out of whose hills thou mayest dig brass" (Deuteronomy 8:9KJV).

"Yea, forty years didst thou sustain them in the wilderness, so that they lacked nothing; their clothes waxed not old, and their feet swelled not" (Nehemiah 9:21KJV).

"The young lions do lack, and suffer hunger: but they that seek the Lord shall not want any good thing" (Psalm 34:10KJV).

Regardless of what you face, a situation or circumstance will appear as if it's bleak, and lack has shown up at your door—but don't invite it in. We must learn as David did that facts are not the determining element in all situations. Truth is. This must be our confession: Nothing broken, nothing missing, nothing lacking. There is no shortage in my home, business, marriage, family, job, or in my health. Everything I need, I can find in Christ. *"And my God shall supply all your need according to His riches in Glory by Christ Jesus"(Philippians 4:19 NKJV).*

Chapter 7: Lord, Your Word Has Made Me Whole

Can you believe that? Does your situation seem impossible? Has someone told you that what you believe God for is doomed for failure? Is your bank account all dried up? Has the doctor given you only weeks, months, or a few years to live? I encourage you this day to believe what the Word says about your future. In Jeremiah 29:11 *(KJV)*, the Bible states, *"For I know the thoughts that I think toward you, saith the LORD, thoughts of peace, and not of evil, to give you an expected end"*

Prayer

Father, I thank You for making it possible to live a life of wholeness, free from the elements of life that would try to contaminate me. Thank You for giving me Your Word to stand on when faced with the difficulties of life. I have complete confidence in Your Word to keep, maintain, and sustain me in every area of my life. I have made a conscience decision to rely on the power of Your Word in every situation I face.

I realize that people or material possession cannot make me complete. I am only complete when I live my life according to Your Word. Just like the woman with the issue of blood, I have tried everything to find true happiness. I realize now that what I was looking for has been there all along. Thank You for making me whole and complete. I lack nothing, regardless of how my outward condition may present itself.

Today's confession: I live this day by trusting and believing in only Your Word. I thank You for making me a complete person by the power of Your unchanging Word.

CHAPTER 8
Lord, Faith In You Has Made Me Whole

"God is not a man that He should tell or act a lie, neither the son of man, that He should feel repentance or compunction for what He has promised]. Has He said and shall He not do it? Or has He spoken and shall He not make it good"? (Numbers 23:19AMP)

People put a lot of trust and reliance in so many things such as the stock market, the economy, jobs, people, family, doctors, lawyers, cars, or money. I guarantee, people will let you down and disappoint you. We have a tendency to put high expectations on others. We expect them to react, respond, and do exactly what we want and when we want. And when they do not measure up to our expectations, we think there is something wrong with *them*.

On the contrary, there is nothing wrong with the individuals, but there is undeniably something wrong with us. People who call themselves perfectionist have this problem. They think they are perfect, and that everything they do is done with quality and excellence. Don't get me wrong. I believe we should do things in excellence, but some people go over board. Do you know someone whose house is spotless? There are no newspapers on the floor, no dishes in the sink, and the bathroom is immaculate. The house is so clean, you wonder if you can even sit on the couch or use their bathroom! They wash their car every other day, and you may never see them wearing the same clothes twice.

These individuals have a zero tolerance for mistakes, and can find it very difficult to accept people who have faults and flaws. It is very hard for perfectionist to admit when they make mistakes. They undoubtedly tend to believe that the mistake was done by someone or something else. They surely are not to blame.

Understanding and knowing the complexities of people, our expectations must always be on Christ. He is someone who's reliable, trustworthy, and according to the above Scripture, He never lies. Christ has not only proven His ability to do what He has promised, but His Word will never fail.

In this passage of Scripture, the writer makes it perfectly clear the difference between Christ and man. The first thing the writer points out is that God is not a man who should lie. Without a doubt, people lie. And many will lie directly to your face and without hesitation. Sometimes you can tell if someone is lying, because they cannot look you right in the eyes (the eyes say a lot about

Chapter 8: Lord, Faith In You Has Made Me Whole

an individual.) People who lie are influenced by the devil. The Bible calls Satan the father of lies, meaning that lies originated from the pit of hell.

> *"You are of your father, the devil, and it is your will to practice the lusts and gratify the desires [which are characteristic] of your father. He was a murderer from the beginning and does not stand in the truth, because there is no truth in him. When he speaks a falsehood, he speaks what is natural to him, for he is a liar [himself] and the father of lies and of all that is false" (John 8:44 AMP).*

Do you realize that if someone is capable of telling one lie, they are capable of lying again? Unfortunately, they will. Did you catch that? This passage states that when the devil speaks lies, it's natural for him to do so. It's a common thing, and one must expect him to do what is in him. "Once a liar always a liar," someone once said. Let the truth be told. The only person that can deliver you from possessing a lying spirit is Christ. Truth is in the nature and character of God.

This statement should leave no misgivings. God will not act, behave, or do anything outside His character. God puts His reputation on the line, and He will back up everything He promised. When God makes a promise, His very Word provides the confirmation. A confirmation assures and gives proof of the transaction and conversation. It's a validation that something occurred.

There must be some valid reason that the writer emphasized this. I believe the writer didn't want anyone to believe that Christ and man had the same nature or character. When I was growing up, people who made promises and went back on their words were called "Indian givers." I'm not sure where this originated from, but we knew exactly what it meant. We should be encouraged, knowing that God will not lie nor renege on His promises. Everything God has promised us will surely come to pass! We must learn to be patient and wait. *"That ye be not slothful, but followers of them who through faith and patience inherit the promises" (Hebrews 6:12KJV).*

Next, the writer says God does not feel repentance or compulsion. Compulsion means to feel regret, to have a second thought, hesitation and to be reluctant. When God makes a promise, He is fully aware that the only person needing to honor the promise is Him.

> *"For when God made promise to Abraham, because he could swear by no greater, he sware by himself, saying, surely blessing I will bless thee, and multiplying I will multiply thee. And so, after he had patiently endured, he obtained the promise. For men verily swear by the greater: and an oath for confirmation is to them an end of all strife. Wherein God, willing more abundantly to shew unto the heirs of promise the immutability of his counsel,*

Chapter 8: Lord, Faith In You Has Made Me Whole

confirmed it by an oath: that by two immutable things, in which it was impossible for God to lie, we might have a strong consolation, who have fled for refuge to lay hold upon the hope set before us" (Hebrews 6:13-18 KJV).

The Promise to Abraham and Sarah

"And behold, the word of the Lord came to him, saying, This man shall not be your heir, but he who shall come from your own body shall be your heir" (Genesis 15:4 AMP).

"And I will bless her, and give thee a son also of her: yea, I will bless her, and she shall be a mother of nations; kings of people shall be of her. Then Abraham fell upon his face, and laughed, and said in his heart, Shall a child be born unto him that is an hundred years old? And shall Sarah, that is ninety years old, bear? And Abraham said unto God, O that Ishmael might live before thee! "And God said Sarah thy wife shall bear thee a son indeed; and thou shalt call his name Isaac: and I will establish my covenant with him for an everlasting covenant and with his seed after him" (Genesis 17:16-19KJV).

"And he said, I will certainly return unto thee according to the time of life; and, lo, Sarah

thy wife shall have a son. And Sarah heard it in the tent door, which was behind him. Now Abraham and Sarah were old and well stricken in age; and it ceased to be with Sarah after the manner of women" (Genesis 18:10-11 KJV).

"Is any thing too hard for the LORD? At the time appointed I will return unto thee, according to the time of life, and Sarah shall have a son" (Genesis 18: 14 KJV).

God is Faithful to Abraham and Sarah

"And the LORD visited Sarah as he had said, and the LORD did unto Sarah as he had spoken. For Sarah conceived, and bare Abraham a son in his old age, at the set time of which God had spoken to him. And Abraham called the name of his son that was born unto him, whom Sarah bare to him, Isaac" (Genesis 21:1-4 KJV).

What a promise! Sometimes believing for bigger things requires more faith and patience. Waiting is the hardest thing to do, especially when God gives you a promise that seems so irrational and far-fetched. Would it be just a little crazy to believe God could bless Abraham and Sarah when this promise seemed irrational? Such a promise was inconceivable, unthinkable, and illogical. A promise like that didn't make any sense. How could God bless Abraham and Sarah with a son when all odds were stacked completely against them? You must believe, even when it goes against all logical thinking. *"For with*

Chapter 8: Lord, Faith In You Has Made Me Whole

God nothing is ever impossible and no word from God shall be without power or impossible of fulfillment" (Luke 1:37 AMP).

Let me reiterate; sometimes things just won't make sense. It's easier for one to believe when one can see, but your faith requires you to believe without having reality staring you in the face. Right here is where reliance, trust, and faith come in. When God gave the promise to Abraham and Sarah, He wasn't expecting them to fulfill the promise. He only wanted to use them as the catalyst in which nations and kings would be birthed.

When it comes to your believing, it has nothing to do with your intelligence, skills, or abilities. The wonderful results God is looking for come strictly from Heaven. He is the only One that produces God-given results such as this. Any promise you receive from God depends on your faith.

"Because of faith also Sarah herself received physical power to conceive a child, even when she was long past the age for it, because she considered [God] Who had given her the promise to be reliable and trustworthy and true to His word" (Hebrews 11:11 AMP).

"By faith Abraham, when he was put to the test [while the testing of his faith was still in progress], had already brought Isaac for an offering; he who had gladly received and welcomed [God's] promises was ready to sacrifice his only son" (Hebrews 17:11 AMP).

"Because of faith the walls of Jericho fell down after they had been encompassed for seven days [by the Israelites]" (Hebrews 11:30 AMP).

The Promise to Mary

"Now in the sixth month [after that], the angel Gabriel was sent from God to a town of Galilee named Nazareth, To a girl never having been married and a virgin engaged to be married to a man whose name was Joseph, a descendant of the house of David; and the virgin's name was Mary."

"And he came to her and said, Hail, O favored one endued with grace! The Lord is with you! Blessed (favored of God) are you before all other women! But when she saw him, she was greatly troubled and disturbed and confused at what he said and kept revolving in her mind what such a greeting might mean. And the angel said to her, Do not be afraid, Mary, for you have found grace free, spontaneous, absolute favor and loving-kindness) with God. And listen! You will become pregnant and will give birth to a Son, and you shall call His name Jesus" (Luke 1:26-31 AMP).

God is Faithful to Mary

"And she gave birth to her Son, her Firstborn; and she wrapped Him in swaddling clothes and laid Him in a manger, because there was

Chapter 8: Lord, Faith In You Has Made Me Whole

no room or place for them in the inn" (Luke 2:7 AMP).

Make sure your confidence does not lie in man. If man has promised you something, and he doesn't make good on the promise, shake the dust off and keep pushing! Don't get hung up on the fact that he either lied, or something came up that made it difficult for him to fulfill the promise. Nevertheless, forgive them, and remember God is not man; He will back up His promise. My faith, hope, and trust must be in Christ. I can be assured what He has promised will come to pass. *"For all the promises of God in him are yea, and in him Amen, unto the glory of God by us" (II Corinthians 1:20 KJV).*

The search and the wait are finally over. Finding someone to meet all your needs, desires, and wants will only come through Christ. Christ is all one needs. He is the source of life, hope, and fulfillment. Other people cannot help you the way Christ can; there is no comparison. Christ brings stability in life. He is the foundation in which one can build its expectation, anticipation, and dependence on. And He shall be called…

The Author of Life: (Acts 3:15 AMP).

"But you killed the very Source (the Author) of life, Whom God raised from the dead. To this we are witnesses"

The Bread of Life: (John 6:35-36 AMP).

"Jesus replied, I am the Bread of Life. He who comes to Me will never be hungry, and he who believes in and cleaves to and trusts in and relies on Me will never thirst any more (at any time)"

Loyal and True: (Revelation 19:11 AMP).

"After that I saw heaven opened, and behold, a white horse [appeared]! The One Who was riding it is called Faithful (Trustworthy, Loyal, Incorruptible, Steady) and True, and He passes judgment and wages war in righteousness (holiness, justice, and uprightness)"

Our Hope: (1 Timothy 1:1 AMP).

"Paul, an apostle (special messenger) of Christ Jesus by appointment and command of God our Savior and of Christ Jesus (the Messiah), our Hope"

Life Giver: (John 14:6 AMP).

"Jesus said to him, I am the Way and the Truth and the Life; no one comes to the Father except by (through) Me"

Faithful: (2 Thessalonians 3:3 AMP).

"Yet the Lord is faithful, and He will strengthen [you] and set you on a firm foundation and guard you from the evil [one]"

Chapter 8: Lord, Faith In You Has Made Me Whole

Prayer

Father, I come to You in the name of Jesus. Thank You that You have committed Yourself to me by making me whole and complete in You. You remain faithful to Your promises, which will never be broken. My search for happiness, success and love comes only from You. People will never measure up to You; therefore, I put all my trust in Your faithfulness. Becoming whole, full and satisfied comes from who You are. Faith in You is all I need for success and happiness. Father, fulfill Your promises in my life this day.

Today's confession: I declare and decree this day that I am complete by my faith in Christ alone.

CHAPTER 9
Lord, Still I Rise

"Five times I received from [the hands of] the Jews forty [lashes all] but one;

Three times I have been beaten with rods; once I was stoned. Three times I have been aboard a ship wrecked at sea; a [whole] night and a day I have spent [adrift] on the deep;

Many times on journeys, [exposed to] perils from rivers, perils from bandits, perils from [my own] nation, perils from the Gentiles, perils in the city, perils in the desert places, perils in the sea, perils from those posing as believers [but destitute of Christian knowledge and piety]; In toil and hardship, watching often [through sleepless nights], in hunger and thirst, frequently driven to fasting by want, in cold and exposure and lack of clothing. And besides those things that are without, there is the daily

Chapter 9: Lord, Still I Rise

[inescapable pressure] of my care and anxiety for all the churches" (II Corinthians 11:24-28 AMP).

How do you see yourself? If all that you have encountered does not push, motivate, and drive you forward, you have failed your test. Your testimony may not be like Paul's, but you do have one. No one knows the magnitude of your pain and sorrows, but I'm convinced if you measured it up to Paul's, it wouldn't come close. However, only you and God know your story.

What Is Your Story?

I've been beaten, scorned and battered because they are intimidated... Still I Rise.
I've been labeled as common and ordinary, because you assume to know me... Still I Rise.
You crush my spirit and break my heart... Still I Rise.
Controlled by people... Still I Rise.
Homeless and sleeping in parks or where ever I could find shelter... Still I Rise.
Faced death by gun fire...Still I Rise.
Storm, rain, and floods... Still I Rise.
In debt, discouraged, and broke... Still I Rise.
Adversities come to wipe me out ... Still I Rise.
Struggling with drugs and alcohol ... Still I Rise.
Accusations, vocal assaults... Still I Rise.
The enemy has set traps to trip me up... Still I Rise.
Mountains, hurdles, obstacles stand in my way... Still I

Rise.
Satan comes to kill, destroy, and steal… Still I Rise.
Lost everything… Still I Rise.
Catastrophe, testing, and trials come… Still I Rise.
You try to suppress me, because you see my determination and spirit … Still I Rise.
Suffering because of my faith… Still I Rise.
Hated because I stand against unrighteousness… Still I Rise.
Misunderstood because I choose to live right, act right, and do right… Still I Rise.
You judge me, because you think I'm arrogant and conceited… Still I Rise.
You can hate on me all your want… Still I rise.
Molested by my family… Still I rise.
In distress and perils on every side…Still I rise.

> *"Watch this: God's eye is on those who respect him, the ones who are looking for his love. He's ready to come to their rescue in bad times; in lean times he keeps body and soul together" (Psalms 33:18-19 MSG).*

I'm not ignorant to the fact that these things occur; nor do I pretend like they have not affected me emotionally, mentally, or physically. To do this would be absurd; however, how I choose to handle these events in my life, depends totally on me. How I overcome is determined by my approach, my character, and my spirit. The same Spirit that kept Paul rising in the midst of difficulty is the

Chapter 9: Lord, Still I Rise

same Spirit that is holding you up. The Spirit of God is resistant to defeat and loss. When you rely on the Spirit in you, you can hold your ground in the midst of conflict, war, and hostility. God will sustain you even when it appears like you're weakening under the pressure. "*Do not panic, God will give you the power to stay calm in the days of adversity*" *(Psalms 94:13 AMP).*

I Possess A Different Spirit

"They came to Moses and Aaron and to all the Israelite congregation in the Wilderness of Paran at Kadesh, and brought them word, and showed them the land's fruit. They told Moses, We came to the land to which you sent us; surely it flows with milk and honey. This is its fruit. But the people who dwell there are strong, and the cities are fortified and very large; moreover, there we saw the sons of Anak [of great stature and courage].

Amalek dwells in the land of the South (the Negeb); the Hittite, the Jebusite, and the Amorite dwell in the hill country; and the Canaanite dwells by the sea and along by the side of the Jordan [River]. Caleb quieted the people before Moses, and said, Let us go up at once and possess it; we are well able to conquer it.

But his fellow scouts said, we are not able to

> *go up against the people [of Canaan], for they are stronger than we are. So they brought the Israelites an evil report of the land which they had scouted out, saying, the land through which we went to spy it out is a land that devours its inhabitants. And all the people that we saw in it are men of great stature. There we saw the Nephilim [or giants], the sons of Anak, who come from the giants; and we were in our own sight as grasshoppers, and so we were in their sight" (Numbers 13:26-33 AMP).*
>
> *"But My servant Caleb, because he has a different spirit and has followed Me fully, I will bring into the land into which he went, and his descendants shall possess it" (Numbers 14:24 AMP).*

Praise God for Caleb, a man who decided not to look at the opposition larger than His God. Caleb did not refute that the people were in the land; nor did he deny that the land was occupied by forces of great strength; yet, Caleb chose not to look through natural spectacles as the fellow scouts. Through the natural eyes, the fellow scouts looked at the size of the people, how fortified the land was, and fear settled in their hearts.

The evil report, therefore, was determined by their inability to see God bigger than the problems before them. Consequently, conquering the land was no option. Caleb and the fellow scouts saw the same people, land, and environment; yet, because Caleb possessed a different spirit, his focus was not on the negative. His focus was on how good the land was—a land flowing with milk and honey. Caleb believed that if God brought them to this place, surely God would allow them to posses the land.

Regardless of the many signs and wonders God will perform, there will always be a people who refuse to trust, rely, and believe God. God is looking for a remnant of people who will look at what is before them and see it as small compared to the greatness and awesomeness of God. In order for you to rise and possess what God has promised you, you must have a different spirit. If you think you can't climb out of your mess, you can't. If you think your circumstances are too big for God, they are. If you believe God does not want you to prosper, you won't. Whatever you believe is what will happen.

You must have a better attitude about yourself, your future, and life. The mental image of your success must be in the forefront of your thoughts. You have what it takes to rise above and come out of the darkness that tries to plague your life!

The Promise of God

"Many evils confront the [consistently] righteous, but the Lord delivers him out of them all" (Psalms 34:19 AMP).

God creates different roads for each of us. Some roads are more difficult to ride. God allows certain people to endure more hardship, perils, and sorrows. Though the path might be difficult, this is the way in which God has designed for people to find the results that only come from experiencing the flat tires, wreaks, and blow outs of life. There is a road map that God has that will take people to new journeys and adventures. Getting to this place of new heights will test your ability and endurance.

I don't know why some of what Paul went through didn't kill him; yet, I know those perils came to do just that. God kept preserving Paul's life, and God has kept you through your own perils, while on this journey called life. Paul continued walking with and serving Christ, regardless of the dangers, risk, and the lack of safety he faced. What a testimony to have when faced with a situation that will jeopardize one's life for the sake of deeply held beliefs, morals, and convictions.

Do you see that you are able to rise above the chaos, mess, and drama? You are unlimited, unrestricted, victorious, and a world-overcomer. You must choose to live above everything that would capture and ensnare you. I've been in bondage, and it doesn't feel good. I refuse to return or go back to that place where my feelings, thoughts, and actions were dictated, and controlled by others. Where is that place? That place is called confinement. I was not created to be manipulated and broken. Yet, at times I find myself giving into the pressures that infiltrate my mind. I rise above my situations and circumstances that have come to defeat me, and cause me to retreat because of what I face.

Through every situation, this is my confession: Still I rise.

Chapter 9: Lord, Still I Rise

Prayer

Father, in the name of Jesus, I thank You for keeping me when I didn't want to be kept. I praise You because of Your power and ability to do what no one else can. I exalt You. I glorify You because You are God. I realize that many things could have taken my life, but You have preserved my life for such a time as this. I praise You this day because You have been my strong Foundation, my Stabilizer and my Guide. I'm only able to rise because of You. Thank You for loving me through it all.

Today's confession: I rise so I can become a complete and whole person.

CHAPTER 10
Completely Whole Celebrating Me

"I will confess and praise You for You are fearful and wonderful and for the awful wonder of my birth! Wonderful are Your works, and that my inner self knows right well" (Psalms 139:14 AMP).

I'm celebrating me because I've come to know that I'm all right—regardless of what you think about me, or how you feel towards me. I celebrate that I am a whole person—spirit, soul, and body. I am who I am because of what God has declared about me.

I'm celebrating the woman God has designed, destined, and called me to be. My celebration continues even if you don't want to rejoice with me. I recognize that the celebration only needs a select number of people. These people will celebrate my freedom, my achievements, and my progress, because they are not intimated by my success.

Chapter 10: Completely Whole Celebrating Me

I'm celebrating my freedom. I'm free from the bondage and the oppression of others. People that are not liberated tend to want to harness others that are progressing and moving forward. My celebration comes from years of struggle—struggling with self and the image within. The picture I see now is not the same one I saw years ago.

Because I allowed others to form and shape me; I became who they wanted me to be. But that is no longer the case, praise God! I have been set free from the stigma and the mindset that others try to put on me. I love me. I know-what a statement! If you can't say that about yourself, then something is wrong.

I realize I have issues, and God is still dealing with me about them; however, my issues will never prohibit me from loving the person I've become. I'm celebrating the freedom in my mind. I'm free to be who I am and do what it is I am created to do. What you expect me to give, I cannot. Giving you the world will not cause you to accept me for who I am. I must be happy, content, and satisfied with me. As I look in the mirror, the person I see is one who has come to terms, with her person, character, and spirit. I change on my terms, and my terms only. Embrace my freedom. Come along and ride with me, if you desire. Celebrate my existence, because celebrating me is celebrating the God in me.

Beauty is loving you—just as you are!

I celebrate my independence because my mind is not cluttered with the voices and conversations of what others have said about me. I celebrate my creativity because my creativity is what allows me to break free from the chains that would bind me. I celebrate me, even if you don't understand me or who I am. I will only change for God. I'll celebrate my victories even if no one else celebrates with me. I'll celebrate my accomplishments because I never thought I could. I celebrate my success because God says I can!

Prayer

Father, in the name of Jesus, I thank You for bringing revelation to me concerning my individuality. I accept me for the person You designed me to be. I pray that I continue growing in the person You created. I celebrate my uniqueness, wholeness and freedom because of Christ. Father, I thank You for my freedom. I will never be bound again by others; nor will I allow others to put me in a box.

Today's confession: I'm celebrating the woman I've become. I embrace me.

CHAPTER 11
Completely Whole Fulfilling Purpose

"There's a right time for everything. There's an opportune time to do things, a right time for everything on the earth" (Ecclesiastes 3:1 MSG).

What is purpose? How can I live in my purpose? While it is important to define what purpose is, I believe purpose must start with God. When we acknowledge the reason why we are created, discovering that reason will answer this question: Why are you on earth? When you begin to recognize your purpose for living, it will produce a life that is fulfilled, complete, and satisfying.

How can I live out my purpose without God in the equation? The answer to that question: You can't: A person who insists on leaving God out of the equation will by no means know and understand the true meaning of living. Here is what happens when we keep God out:

"But God's angry displeasure erupts as acts of human mistrust and wrongdoing and lying

accumulate, as people try to put a shroud over truth. But the basic reality of God is plain enough. Open your eyes and there it is! By taking a long and thoughtful look at what God has created, people have always been able to see what their eyes as such can't see: eternal power, for instance, and the mystery of his divine being. So nobody has a good excuse.

What happened was this: people knew God perfectly well, but when they didn't treat Him like God. They refused to worship him; they trivialized themselves into silliness and confusion so that there was neither sense nor direction left in their lives. They pretended to know it all, but were illiterate regarding life. They traded the glory of God who holds the whole world in his hands, for cheap figurines you can buy at any roadside stand" (Romans 1:18-23 MSG).

"So God said, in effect, "If that's what you want, that's what you get." It wasn't long before they were living in a pigpen, smeared with filth, filthy inside and out. And all this because they traded the true God for a fake god, and worshiped the god they made instead of the God who made them—the God we bless, the God who blesses us. Oh, yes"! (Romans 1:24-25 MSG).

"Refusing to know God, they soon didn't know how to be human either—women didn't know

Chapter 11: Completely Whole Fulfilling Purpose

how to be women, men didn't know how to be men. Sexually confused, they abused and defiled one another, women with women, men with men—all lust, no love. And then they paid for it, oh, how they paid for it—emptied of God and love, godless and loveless wretches. Since they didn't bother to acknowledge God, God quit bothering them and let them run loose. And then all hell broke loose: rampant evil, grabbing and grasping, vicious backstabbing. They made life hell on earth with their envy, wanton killing, bickering, and cheating. Look at them: mean-spirited, venomous, fork-tongued God-bashers. Bullies, swaggerers, insufferable windbags! They keep inventing new ways of wrecking lives. They ditch their parents when they get in the way—they're stupid, slimy, cruel, and cold-blooded. And it's not as if they don't know better. They know perfectly well they're spitting in God's face. And they don't care— worse, they hand out prizes to those who do the worst things best"! (Romans 1:26-32 MSG).

When we insist on having our own way or not consulting God, we are prone to fall in error. This passage of Scripture points out several interesting factors:

- No one is without excuse—God has clearly shown His existence. His presence is everywhere.

- There was no reverence of God.
- People pretended to know it all, and there was no need to invite God into any decision-making.

If we try to erase God out of our lives, out of our schools, and government, we are pointing a finger at God and telling Him we don't need Him, which is certainly not true! The danger of this type of attitude is that we are now operating without restraints, protection, and control. Without the guidance of God, there is no vision, direction, or purpose. You cannot fulfill your true purpose in life if you exclude or reject God. Your life will be utterly meaningless.

Life became meaningless because they had rejected God, who is the Giver of all things. It may appear that people who have eliminated God are living a life full of happiness, success, and peace; but inwardly they are lonely and empty.

I realize that many people have achieved great success without acknowledging God, but I don't believe those same people are truly happy. True happiness comes when a person identifies his purpose, and lives his dreams with God in the center of everything he does.

Purpose has many definitions depending on who you ask. To a scientist, fulfilling purpose could be discovering a cure for a rare disease; to a football player, fulfilling purpose could be winning the Super Bowl; to some, it could be graduating from college. Whatever the case may be, purpose is what you live for. For every decision or action you've made in life, purpose somehow has played a vital role.

Purpose for Creation

Everything exists for a purpose or reason. In Genesis 1:1-26 KJV, God created nature for purpose.

> *"In the beginning God created the heaven and the earth. And the earth was without form, and void; and darkness was upon the face of the deep. And the Spirit of God moved upon the face of the waters. And God said, Let there be light: and there was light. And God saw the light, that it was good: and God divided the light from the darkness"*

Creation knows its purpose. Why is it that the very people created in the image of God cannot pinpoint their purposes? Mankind roams aimlessly without purpose or identity. Without direction from its Creator, mankind goes for years wanting to connect and belong to something bigger than itself. Because mankind is unfulfilled and frustrated with life, he subconsciously aborts the visions and dreams that are deeply embedded in its soul. Mankind aborts that which he has no idea he possesses. Because he is unable to come into the full revelation of who and what he possesses, mankind walks on earth not linked with, nor has come into oneness with, himself or God.

Where there is a lack of knowledge regarding purpose, people who have great talents, skills, and abilities do not tap the internal resources needed to live an abundant life. When this happens, some people die without fulfilling their God-given assignment.

The world has not benefited from this person's creative abilities, ideals, or inventions. This person was unable to make a difference in the world because he failed to walk in his divine purpose. Finding true purpose enables a person to make an impact on our nation, country, and people. When a person knows what he is supposed to do on earth, obstacles may attempt to interrupt the process, but the purpose driven individual moves forward, regardless of the circumstances.

Purpose makes us unique. God created us with different personalities, characters, and colors. There are no two people alike. Although twins might be similar in appearance, God did not give them the same fingerprint. God wants us to come into our own sense of personhood. He wants us to be able to discover exactly why we are here and for what reason. No two people were created to do the same things alike. Even though our functions might be alike in nature, how we carry out the call is totally different.

Purpose identified is life's ultimate achievement. When mankind can discover the reason for his existence, his full potential, can be obtained without hesitation. In order for mankind to reach his full potential, he must come into alignment with his Creator. We cannot arrive at a place of full distinctiveness without realizing that it

Chapter 11: Completely Whole Fulfilling Purpose

is God Himself who has created us to live, not apart from Him, but in harmony with Him.

Finding your purpose in life should be one of your greatest goals. For one to fulfill his role and assignment here on earth, one must be aware of his own skills, talents, and abilities. Mankind must be aware of his own personality and how his personality fits into the purpose for which he was created. You are who you are by divine design. No one person has the right to try to change you to fit who they think you should be. God created you differently for the sole purpose of fitting you into the right place, vocation, city, family, and church.

Purpose is fulfilled through life's experiences. Some of life's challenges and struggles lead us to God's divine purpose and plan for our lives.

Running Away From God (Jonah 1 MSG)

"One day long ago, God's Word came to Jonah, Amittai's son: "Up on your feet and on your way to the big city of Nineveh! Preach to them. They're in a bad way and I can't ignore it any longer." But Jonah got up and went the other direction to Tarshish, running away from God. He went down to the port of Joppa and found a ship headed for Tarshish. He paid the fare and went on board, joining those going to Tarshish—as far away from God as he could get.

"But God sent a huge storm at sea, the waves towering. At that, the men were frightened, really frightened, and said, "What on earth have you done!" As Jonah talked, the sailors realized that he was running away from God. Jonah said, "Throw me overboard, into the sea. Then the storm will stop. It's all my fault. I'm the cause of the storm. Get rid of me and you'll get rid of the storm." They took Jonah and threw him overboard. Immediately the sea was quieted down.

"The sailors were impressed, no longer terrified by the sea, but in awe of God. They worshiped God, offered a sacrifice, and made vows. Then God assigned a huge fish to swallow Jonah. Jonah was in the fish's belly three days and nights."

"Then Jonah prayed to the Lord his God from the fish's belly" (Jonah 2 MSG).

"And the word of the Lord came to Jonah the second time, saying, Arise, go to Nineveh, that great city, and preach and cry out to it the preaching that I tell you. So Jonah arose and went to Nineveh according to the word of the Lord. Now Nineveh was an exceedingly great city of three days' journey [sixty miles in circumference]" (Jonah 3 AMP).

Chapter 11: Completely Whole Fulfilling Purpose

When God has given us an assignment, no matter how hard we try to run and avoid it, we can't. Jonah is the prime example. Jonah's purpose was to preach. Jonah made it perfectly clear to God that he didn't want to see Nineveh delivered. Jonah did everything in his strength and power to run away from the plan, purpose, and will of God. Jonah's act of disobedience almost cost the sailors their lives. The Scripture records that Jonah went in another direction. I don't know why Jonah thought he could hide and escape from the presence of the Lord because God is everywhere!

One is led to believe that Jonah was on the right course until God told him to go preach and bring deliverance to Nineveh—an assignment he was not willing to accept. Nevertheless, Jonah finally came to his senses when the Lord caused the violent sea storm. God had a purpose for Jonah in Nineveh. Jonah was the key to the whole city coming to repentance, and God granted Jonah a second chance to preach the message of deliverance. As a result of these events, Nineveh believed in God and repented.

This is such a powerful story of how one person's divine purpose in life touched not only a city, but the heart of God. The king declared a fast for the entire nation and declared that everyone turn from evil and violence. The Scriptures record that God saw their good works, and God revoked His judgment upon them. What a turn around! A city headed for destruction was given another opportunity to live right before God.

Do you realize that people are connected to your divine purpose? You have the very keys and answers that people need and are waiting for. Someone is waiting in the valley of decision for you. Someone has been assigned to help you in your purpose, and you have been assigned to help someone with their vision or dream. Just as Nineveh was prepared for Jonah, God is preparing a people, nation, job, family, and church for you to come fulfill your purpose in the earth.

What are you waiting for? Believe it or not, we need each other to fulfill the purpose for which we exist; we can't fulfill purpose alone. The vision that God gives an individual is too large for one person to fulfill. Someone has a skill or talent that you need in order to complete the assignment that God has given you. The areas that you are weak in, God will raise up someone that is stronger in that area to assist you so your job will not be unbearable. Realizing that someone is waiting to assist us in doing what God has called us to do may bring added pressure; nevertheless, you can't sit back knowing that someone is waiting on you to fulfill purpose. Take others with you as you find out exactly what it is that drives you to success.

Fulfilling purpose creates successful people, and successful people create opportunities for others to be successful. In other words, my success opens up doors for others. I don't want to be the only person benefiting from what God does in my life; I want to share that with others so they, too, can reproduce after their kind!

Are you running away from God like Jonah? Is there something God is telling you to do and you refuse? Did Jonah think this task was too big for him? Whatever it may be, God's purpose and plan will be fulfilled. *"Many*

Chapter 11: Completely Whole Fulfilling Purpose

plans are in a man's mind, but it is the Lord's purpose for him that will stand" (Proverbs 19:21 AMP).

Fulfilling purpose is your choice. When opportunities come, the choice will be yours to either accept the proposal or reject it. Most times we reject great opportunities because they look too big for us to achieve. In most cases, they are. Our natural instinct is to pass on those opportunities because we look within ourselves knowing that we do not have the capabilities to do something that is so great. We rationalize the idea that God could be presenting this before us to thrust us into His purpose and will for our lives. We think, "Could God choose me to do something that I haven't done before?"

If this is the scenario you are facing, remember God is looking for your obedience and trust. He realizes that you feel incapable of carrying out such a tremendous task; yet, this is the very reason He has chosen you for this particular assignment. Your dependency and reliance has to be on Him. It is in moments like these that God will begin to prove and make obvious His power working in and through you. Fulfilling the purposes of God should be your utmost desire.

If God has selected you for this assignment, know this: God has obligated Himself to give you what you need to fulfill the task without worry or stress. Accept the assignment boldly, for it is with great purpose that God has chosen this for you. Understand that purpose produces passion, and passion must be the driving force behind you fulfilling your dreams, goals, and desires. Everywhere you go, this will be your conversation.

Everywhere you go, your passion and what you believe in will be evident in your speech or action. Purpose will cause you to look for opportunities to fulfill your passion. Pursue with earnest zeal God's plan for your life, and embrace the purpose for which you were born. Fulfilling divine purpose will cause you to live a complete, satisfying, and enjoyable life.

Fulfilling The Purpose Of Others

No one can change the person you are meant to be. People will try to live their dreams, aspirations, and hopes through you. If you don't discover your purpose for living, people will impose their purpose on you. While people may not realize the detrimental and long-lasting effects this may have on a person, living your purpose through others is selfish. I have heard my share of stories in which a parent who didn't graduate from college or achieve some type of success tried to push their children into achieving something they were unable to accomplish themselves.

Not encouraging the child to develop into his person, and discover his purpose for living, leads the child to journey in a direction that does not bring him joy, fulfillment, or happiness. The child grows up with bitterness in his heart towards his parents for not allowing him to pursue his own personal desires, dreams, goals, and aspirations. A life with great potential and possibilities is now unfulfilled and empty. What can you do? Refuse to let others determine purpose for you. Your goal in life is to identify who you are. Be pleased with the person God intended you to become. Even when others are disappointed in you or with the decisions you make, true happiness can only be obtained by you fulfilling your purpose in life. In two words: Do you!

Finding Purpose Now

Are you living in your right time? Have you recognized that you are living in your divine purpose? God has designed a specific plan and purpose for your life. He has plans that are full of exciting moments—moments that are unforgettable, amazing, and worthy of taking note! These moments are both life-changing and life-altering. These are moments of divine appointments and connections with people that will help propel you into destiny.

You must recognize your moment, and seize every opportunity to excel and advance with great momentum. Purpose revealed is success achieved. If you are blinded or short-sighted by the elements of the world, and you have no idea what to do or why you are here, time will pass you by. Ask yourself, are you doing what you enjoy? Have you let time tick away without taking full advantage of all that is intended for you?

Wasted years cannot be restored; nor can you go back and redo years of idleness. You must know that this is your time to do the things that will bring happiness to your life and the lives of others. Do you realize that time waits for no one? Regardless of when you find life and do those things that are pleasing to you, time continues to march on. The purpose of time is to give you the opportunities to do something rewarding and satisfying. God gives us time to enjoy life and to make a difference in the lives of others. You must take full advantage of every moment that is given to you and live life to the fullest. Realize that God has given you time to complete and pursue the purpose for which you were created.

Fulfilling your purpose takes commitment. You are on earth to make a change in your community, home, school, government, and job. Finding purpose can change everything around you. God did not create you to sit still and do nothing. There is so much that needs to be done, and you have the necessary tools, skills, and ability to carry out the assignment. No other person can fulfill your purpose except you. People need what you have. You have something to offer to everyone you come in contact with; you have been assigned to someone. God has someone whose life you are supposed to touch by whatever you are called to do. You will find out who they are when you fulfill your true purpose for living.

Prayer

Father, I come before You in the name of Jesus. I want to thank You for revealing my divine purpose for my life. I know I have not been put on earth for nothing. I have been called to make a difference in someone's life. Lord, thank You for removing the veil from my eyes so that I can see why You put me here. Reveal Your purpose

Chapter 11: Completely Whole Fulfilling Purpose

to all those that call You Father. Fulfill Your purpose in the lives of Your children. May people come to recognize that true happiness can only be obtained by having a genuine relationship with Christ.

Today's confession: I am fulfilling my purpose in life and I am completely whole.

CHAPTER 12
Completely Whole
I'm Willing to Endure

"Persecutions, afflictions, which came unto me at Antioch, at Iconium, at Lystra; what persecutions I endured: but out of them all the Lord delivered me" (II Timothy 3:22 KJV).

Are you enduring for a greater purpose? A person must first know what that greater purpose is. Until a person comes to understand that, their tests and trials won't make any sense. Frustration will settle in the hearts of those who fail to recognize that we must learn to endure the difficulties in life. Many times people give up on a dream or vision right before the breakthrough. A person who is able to endure through affliction, no doubt, is someone who has learned how to fight. In order for Christ to complete His work in your life, you must be willing to endure the hardships you will face while serving God.

"And after you have suffered a little while, the God of all grace [Who imparts all blessing and

Chapter 12: Completely Whole I'm Willing to Endure

favor], Who has called you to His [own] eternal glory in Christ Jesus, will Himself complete and make you what you ought to be, establish and ground you securely, and strengthen, and settle you" (1 Peter 5:10 AMP).

It is not *before* the suffering that you become more like Christ; but Peter is saying it is *after* you suffer. There goes that word again...suffering. Suffering is to experience something unpleasant. It is something that causes pain and affliction.

Who on earth likes to suffer? No one likes the pain of suffering; however, there is something that happens to a person when he suffers, especially suffering for Christ. It is through the suffering that the image of Christ is manifested in our lives. More of His character is revealed through the greatest hours of hardships, perplexities, and distresses. While becoming a whole and complete person, God will put tests and trials before you. How you handle those trials is totally up to you.

Let's examine each word that Peter uses in this passage. First, he says Christ will complete you. The dictionary defines "complete" as "lacking nothing, entire, to make thorough, perfect and without defect." Usually, when we are facing a test or trial, we tend to confess the wrong things. What comes out of our mouths is what the enemy has shown us.

For example, if the money in your checkbook is low, you confess you don't have any money. Or if the doctor has given you a bad report, you confess what the doctor has said. At all times, especially during times of great difficulty, our confession must be the Word of God. Just as Jesus spoke the Word to Satan in the wilderness, we must confess the Word of God over every situation that does not line up with what God has said. Here's an illustration of the test:

> *"Next Jesus was taken into the wild by the Spirit for "the test." The Devil was ready to give it. Jesus prepared for "the test" by fasting forty days and forty nights. That left him, of course, in a state of extreme hunger, which the Devil took advantage of in the first test: "Since you are God's Son, speak the word that will turn these stones into loaves of bread." Jesus answered by quoting Deuteronomy: "And He humbled you and allowed you to hunger and fed you with manna, which you did not know nor did your fathers know, that He might make you recognize and personally know that man does not live by bread only, but man lives by every word that proceeds out of the mouth of the Lord" (Deuteronomy 8:3 AMP).*

> *"For the second test the Devil took him to the Holy City. He sat him on top of the Temple and said, "Since you are God's Son, jump." The Devil goaded him by quoting Psalm 91: "He has placed you in the care of angels. They will catch you so that you won't so much as stub*

Chapter 12: Completely Whole I'm Willing to Endure

your toe on a stone." Jesus countered with another citation from Deuteronomy: "Don't you dare test the Lord your God" (Matthew 4:3-7 MSG).

Just as Jesus was tested to speak against the Word of God, you, too, will be tested. Jesus gives us the greatest example of what we should be speaking when faced with severe and tremendous challenges. There will always be intense pressure to violate the teaching of the Bible when opposition comes in full force, but remain faithful to what you have been taught. Once the enemy realizes that you will not be moved from the truth, he will flee. "*So be subject to God. Resist the devil [stand firm against him], and he will flee from you" (James 4:7 AMP).*

While the test is before me and things appear wrong, I will not allow my words to disagree with the Scriptures. Peter then goes on to say that Christ will make us what we ought to be. Although the Amplified Bible uses the phrase "ought to be," the King James uses the word "perfect." We will examine both terms.

God is working on me in the process of my suffering. Old patterns and mindsets are being removed from my life. The old man is going through a metamorphosis. Metamorphosis is a change of form, shape, structure, or substance; it's a transformation, a mark or complete change of character, appearance, or condition. Although humans grow naturally and insects grow in stages, a comparison will take place between the stages of a butterfly, and the spiritual stages of believers. First let's look at the stages of a butterfly.

Complete metamorphosis for an insect has four stages: **egg**, **larva**, **pupa** and **adult**. Every insect begins life as an egg. The egg is the embryo stage. The larva hatches from the egg. The larva (plural: **larvae**) is the eating and growing stage. Some insects don't eat at all after this stage. Larvae don't look like adults. Caterpillars, grubs, and maggots are larvae that grow up to be butterflies, beetles, and flies as adults. A larva's exoskeleton can't stretch or grow, so the larva sheds its skin, or molts, several times as it grows.

When a larva has finished growing, it forms a pupa (plural: **pupae**). The pupa is the insect's transforming stage. Outside, the pupa looks as if it's resting. But inside, the entire body is rearranging—new organs, muscles and body parts develop. When it has finished changing, the pupa molts one last time, emerging as an adult. The adult is the reproductive stage. The adult has all the identifiable insect features: three body sections, six legs, two antennae and usually wings.

Spiritual Stages Of The Believer

When we are born again, our spirit becomes alive to God. Our spirit must begin to grow by studying the Word, spending time with God in prayer, and attending church. The egg in the butterfly is like the Word, or seed, to the believer. This is how life begins for the believer with a seed. Let's examine how we are to grow. When a person hears the Word, but have not allowed the Word to cultivate his heart, the devil will come and snatch that

Chapter 12: Completely Whole I'm Willing to Endure

was given. When the Word is only heard and not applied to the lives of individuals, Satan comes and prevents it from having any affect in the heart of people. Because the individual has no understanding or revelation of the Word of God, it's easy for Satan to take what has no time to develop and grow. These are the ones that fall by the wayside. *"Those by the way side are they that hear; then cometh the devil, and taketh away the word out of their hearts, lest they should believe and be saved" (Luke 8:12).*

It is vital to your growth as a child of God to keep and harness the Word in times of great need. A lack of understanding of the true meaning of certain Scriptures will hinder you, especially when faced with a situation that requires you to stand on the Word. If we discard the very Word that is preached, a test will come, and we will not have any support to keep us standing while under trial. *"Ignore the Word and suffer; honor God's commands and grow rich" (Proverbs 13:11-13 MSG).*

Next Jesus describes the stony ground:

"They on the rock are they, which, when they hear, receive the word with joy; and these have no root, which for a while believe, and in time of temptation fall away"(Luke 8:13 KJV).

The stony ground represents those who hear the Word, rejoice, and accept it until it is tested in their lives. Because they have not allowed the Word to take root in them, when tribulations arise for the Word's sake, they stumble. Instead of permitting it to carry them through the tribulations, their faith crumbles at the moment of testing. These types of people believe only while things are going well, or when they aren't faced with any current challenges that would require them to stay committed to the faith.

> *"As for God, His way is perfect! The word of the Lord is tested and tried; He is a shield to all those who take refuge and put their trust in Him. For who is God except the Lord? Or who is the Rock save our God, the God who girds me with strength and makes my way perfect? He makes my feet like hinds' feet [able to stand firmly or make progress on the dangerous heights of testing and trouble]; He sets me securely upon my high places"(Psalms 18:30-33 AMP).*

> *"And that which fell among thorns are they, which, when they have heard, go forth, and are choked with cares and riches and pleasures of this life, and bring no fruit to perfection" (Luke 8: 14 KJV).*

The thorny ground depicts those who allow money, and the desire for other things, to choke the Word from bearing any fruit. This type of individual cares about the things of the world and not the things of the Kingdom of God. The desires and pleasures of this life come to distract the individual from pursuing and living a life of

Chapter 12: Completely Whole I'm Willing to Endure

faith. These individuals spend all their time and energy chasing after money while their spiritual life suffers.

"No one can serve two masters; for either he will hate the one and love the other, or he will stand by and be devoted to the one and despise and be against the other. You cannot serve God and mammon (deceitful riches, money, possessions, or whatever is trusted in)" (Matthew 6:24 MSG).

"But that on the good ground are they, which in an honest and good heart, having heard the word, keep it, and bring forth fruit with patience" (Luke 8:15 KJV).

The good ground portrays the one who hears, understands, and receives the Word, and then allows the Word to accomplish its result in his life. The result of hearing, receiving, and applying the Word is a life that bears fruit.

This parable represents the heart of four types of individuals. A man must be receptive to the Word of God, but this is determined by the condition of his heart. The heart of man must be plowed, just as soil is tilled for the farmer. If one's heart is not ready to accept the truth, the individual will go on his merry way, unchanged and untouched by God. God's desire is for everyone to hear, but God knows everyone will not receive. Those who do not receive will live a life unfulfilled and disconnected from his Creator.

Next, let's examine the word "establish." To establish is "to make stable, to make firm." While we are going through the anguish and sorrows, our foundation, which is Christ, will be able to keep us from been tossed to and fro. During hard times, our minds tend to wander off. Staying focused is a challenge because we are too consumed with the pain. Nevertheless, if it is in the plan of God to cause us to become firm and stable in our faith, and if suffering is the way to get us there, then suffering it must be.

Next, let's examine what Peter says about grounding you securely. This is what we desperately need-to be grounded securely. How many times have we allowed circumstances to move us from our faith and position—from a position of safety, confidence, and the promises of God? A foundation that is unstable will never be able to stand against the floods, rains, and storms of life. Once we get the revelation of why God allows sufferings, we will be more willing to accept life with all the changes it brings.

Despite facing some sort of painful experience, you can live a life free from fear, doubt, and worry. You may ask. "How can this be possible?" The answer can be found as you look over your life. The same tests and trials that may have killed someone else have not killed you. While others have succumbed to the pressures of life, you have been resilient—standing firm and unmovable in the face of death, fiery trials, and intense heat.

Suffering is a sure way to cause development and maturity in one's life. It is in the suffering that we are

Chapter 12: Completely Whole I'm Willing to Endure

the most vulnerable; yet, it is here where Christ will become strong in you. *"For when I am weak [in human strength], then am I [truly] strong (able, powerful in divine strength)" (II Corinthians 12:10 AMP).*

Development and maturity are obtained when you have stood your ground under the pressure. Look at the first five letters of pressure: p-r-e-s-s. That is exactly what we must do to survive the suffering, trials, and tests of life. The dictionary defines press as "to push steadily against; squeeze for the purpose of making smooth and compact." When you are under pressure from work, ministry, family, or finances, you must learn to push against those things that come to squeeze the very life out of you. Pressure comes to mature us, but pressure can also take, steal, and destroy our faith. Pressure will either drive you to—or away—from God. If enough pressure is applied, you may begin breaking. This is exactly what the enemy wants to do; he wants to break your spirit. If he is successful in breaking your spirit, he has gotten the victory in your life. Then you will live a defeated life, despite Christ's promise that you will triumph in all things. *"Now thanks be unto God, which always causeth us to triumph in Christ, and maketh manifest the savour of his knowledge by us in every place" (II Corinthians 2:14 KJV).*

When under tremendous stress and worry due to the cares of the world, you must be determined to move your way forward by breaking through the obstacles that come to cause you to stumble. To stumble is merely to fall into sin, to fall into error; it also means to trip or miss one's step in walking or running. This, too, is the desire of Satan—to put people, events, and circumstances, in our way, which will hinder, or cause difficulty while in the pursuit of God.

David's plea for relief from persecutors:

"I cried unto the LORD with my voice; with my voice unto the LORD did I make my supplication"

"I poured out my complaint before him; I shewed before him my trouble"

"When my spirit was overwhelmed within me, then thou knewest my path. In the way wherein I walked have they privily laid a snare for me"

"I looked on my right hand, and beheld, but there was no man that would know me: refuge failed me; no man cared for my soul"

"I cried unto thee, O LORD: I said, Thou art my refuge and my portion in the land of the living"

"Attend unto my cry; for I am brought very low: deliver me from my persecutors; for they are stronger than"

"Bring my soul out of prison, that I may praise thy name: the righteous shall compass me

Chapter 12: Completely Whole I'm Willing to Endure

about; for thou shalt deal bountifully with me" (Psalms 142:1-7 KJV).

Let's examine the structure of this psalm:

David's cry for help in the midst of despair
David acknowledges his trouble
David confesses his spirit is overwhelmed
David recognizes that no one is on his side
David's confession of trust in God
David's petition for deliverance
David's promise to give God praise for his deliverance

Now let's examine David's actions in spite of his distresses. In verse one, he recognizes that God was his only source of deliverance from his persecutors, and so David cries aloud to God. No doubt, David was in deep despair and in desperate need of God to bring him deliverance.

In verse two, David tells God about all his troubles. It's okay to tell God what's wrong; He already knows. Sometimes we get so spiritual that we try not to confess or acknowledge our problems. I'm not saying be a constant complainer; however, when we see that there is a problem, go to the only source that will change your situation. God did not call us to be naïve or ignorant of trouble, problems, or danger. God expects us to see what is wrong, but confess what is right! Use wisdom!

In verse three, David realizes that God knows exactly where he is, and God knows the path David is on. Basically, David tells God, "I know you see me." Although God sees us in places that we do not want to be in, places that cause us pain and heartache, God will leave us there while carrying us through. At times, one may not believe that God is present, but He is. It is here where your faith and trust must be resolved. God is walking with us even when it seems like God has forsaken us. *"Yes, though I walk through the [deep, sunless] valley of the shadow of death, I will fear or dread no evil, for You are with me; Your rod [to protect] and Your staff [to guide], they comfort me"(Psalms 23: 4 AMP).*

In verse four, David realizes that all had forsaken him. Those he thought would be there in his time of emergency and urgency were gone. Have you been there? People you just knew had your back, took off, and left you bleeding and hurting in your condition. Even those good, old saints you once trusted were nowhere to be found. In the greatest times of adversity, you will find out who your real friends are. A genuine and bona fide friend will stick with you in every trial, test, and storm. The only person that won't forsake you is God. He'll stick by you even when you make mistakes, stumble, and fall. Realize that Christ is your source of comfort, your satisfaction, and your substance in which you were created.

Do not look to others to provide what only God can provide. I'm not saying we don't need one another—

Chapter 12: Completely Whole I'm Willing to Endure

we do, but our hope, reliance, and dependence must be primarily on Him. You don't have to keep searching for others to bring you joy or peace. That only comes from the true source of joy and peace—Christ. God is the very breath you breathe. Without Him, we cannot do anything in and of ourselves. *"For in him we live, and move, and have our being" (Acts 17:28 KJV).*

In verse five of Psalms 147, David declares God to be his refuge. The dictionary defines "refuge" as "a person who gives shelter, or protector from danger, a place of safety; safe retreat." In the midst of David's quandary, he renewed his confidence in God, the One who would never leave him. David starts to take his attention from his current situation and towards the truth that lies within. The truth within him knows God to be a refuge, shelter, and protector from every storm. Even in the midst of your pain, you must direct your energy and attention to God. Maybe you should take a moment to reflect on your past victories—victories in which you had no way or idea how you were going to get out of a dilemma. Faced with impossible circumstances and closed doors, God made a way out of no way and delivered you. But God! In the final days, hours, or even seconds, God showed up! How incredible He is! He will allow us to get to a point in our walk with Him to test us, to see how long we can handle the situation without buckling or weakening our faith. And then He steps in—always right on time. He knows exactly when to come to your rescue.

Time and time again, God will continue to show you that if He brought you deliverance and answered your prayers once, He will certainly do it again. At times fear will try to surface, but knowing that God is the One who will protect you, fear will be driven away. Honestly, there is no need to fear or give way to your emotions. Emotions are subject to change and can be untrustworthy. Understand that God will cover you twenty-four-seven. He will provide protection from the elements that come to bring you harm and destruction.

In verse six, David pleads for deliverance from his persecutors. Here David acknowledges his foes are stronger than him. Regardless of how many people come against you, God will defend you. Yes, David cried; he wanted to escape from the hands of his enemies; but he took counsel in knowing that his deliverance was going to come by God. Previous episodes of God coming to his aide are evident in many of the Psalms.

> *"Lord, how are they increased that trouble me! many are they that rise up against me. Many there be which say of my soul, There is no help for him in God. Selah. But thou, O LORD, art a shield for me; my glory, and the lifter up of mine head"(Psalms 3:1-3 KJV).*

> *"The LORD also will be a refuge for the oppressed, a refuge in times of trouble"(Psalms 9:9 KJV).*

> *"The LORD hear thee in the day of trouble; the name of the God of Jacob defend thee"(Psalms 20:1 KJV).*

Chapter 12: Completely Whole I'm Willing to Endure

The Hebrew translation for "trouble" is "adversary, foe, enemy, afflicted, anguish, and distress." David faced much opposition from every side; yet, God never disappointed him when it came to bringing David deliverance. As you walk with God, you, too, will face opposition even from the household of faith. One would think that Christians should rejoice when something good happens to someone else, but on the contrary; jealously, envy, and back biting will surface. Keep your composure and do as David, remembering that God will bring you to a place of total fulfillment as you continue trusting Him during these hard times.

In verse seven, David no doubt is in despair. He acknowledges where he is emotionally and spiritually. His prayer is for God to bring him out of prison so he can offer up praise. Even in the place of turmoil and bondage, David knows what he must do once he is released from prison. Because David is a worshipper, he longs to be in the presence of God. Although at times, we might find ourselves in this predicament, nothing should ever stop our praise, even while we are in uncomfortable places in life. David's promise to God is this: Once God brings him out of prison, David vows to confess, give thanks and praise God. Remember, when you make a promise to God, God is expecting you to keep your word.

Sometimes it is hard to recognize when the enemy put traps before you because he may use the least likely person or thing. These traps are designed by the enemy to trick the unsuspecting person, and to lure them into dangerous, unknown territory. There could be stumbling blocks along the journey, pot holes, or forks in the road. Have you gotten a surprise attack from someone you least expected? If so, you are not alone. Many are experiencing the same troubles. I believe there are people assigned to harass you, but they are actually there to push you forward. I know that might sound unusual, but it is true. If we live life without anyone harassing us, either on our jobs, in our neighborhoods, in our churches and families, we will never realize that we have problems with anger, forgiveness, hatred, self-control, and many other issues. God will allow people to "get under our skin" to show us what areas we need to prune.

Faith Endures

Your faith can only be taken from you when you have focused too much on your pain, problems, and circumstances. You must make a conscious decision to turn from your pain, and focus your thoughts toward the person, works, and wonders of God. When you begin to mediate on the person and the character of God, you will begin to see that what you are facing is little compared to the God you serve. You must exalt your God bigger than your problems, pain and sorrows. Your faith will take you to places that your emotions cannot.

The enemy knows once he bombards you with everything that is going wrong, he will soon get you to doubt the Word of God and His ability to bring you through the trouble. God has promised that if you will not give way to doubt or fear while enduring, you will win.

Chapter 12: Completely Whole I'm Willing to Endure

But Jesus was matter-of-fact:

"Yes—and if you embrace this kingdom life and don't doubt God, you'll not only do minor feats like I did to the fig tree, but also triumph over huge obstacles. This mountain, for instance, you'll tell, 'Go jump in the lake,' and it will jump. Absolutely everything, ranging from small to large, as you make it a part of your believing prayer, gets included as you lay hold of God" (Matthew 21:21 MSG).

Jesus said you will absolutely triumph over everything—and everything means everything. As you lay hold of, embrace, keep, and hold vital the Word of truth, the Word of life that is preached, everything large or small, hard, challenging and impossible will have to line up with the Word of God. Here are a few things one must do while enduring:

- Hold and embrace truth, even when the truth about the matter is not evident
- Find Scriptures that will support what you are believing God for
- Pray in faith, believing that God will answer your request
- Offer up thanksgiving and praise while enduring
- In the day of trouble, seek the Lord
- I know these tips might sound so simple, but you'd be surprise how the simplest things to remember are forgotten while under pressure and facing storms.

Some experiences come to try your temperament and patience. However, if you continue allowing God to enlarge you under these adverse conditions, people will begin to see the Christ in you. What you ought to be will begin to permeate your speech, behavior, and actions. Let your faith move you toward achieving some impossible things that you desire, but have not yet trusted God to bless you with.

The Forth Man In The Fire

"Furious, King Nebuchadnezzar ordered Shadrach, Meshach, and Abednego to be brought in. When the men were brought in, Nebuchadnezzar asked, "Is it true, Shadrach, Meshach, and Abednego, that you don't respect my gods and refuse to worship the gold statue that I have set up? I'm giving you a second chance—but from now on, when the big band strikes up you must go to your knees and worship the statue I have made. If you don't worship it, you will be pitched into a roaring furnace, no questions asked. Who is the god who can rescue you from my power?" Shadrach, Meshach, and Abednego answered King Nebuchadnezzar, "Your threat means nothing to us. If you throw us in the fire, the God we serve can rescue us from your roaring furnace and anything else you might cook up, O king. But even if he

Chapter 12: Completely Whole I'm Willing to Endure

doesn't, it wouldn't make a bit of difference, O king. We still wouldn't serve your gods or worship the gold statue you set up." Suddenly King Nebuchadnezzar jumped up in alarm and said, "Didn't we throw three men, bound hand and foot, into the fire?" "That's right, O king," they said. "But look!" he said. "I see four men, walking around freely in the fire, completely unharmed! And the fourth man looks like a son of the gods"(Daniel 3 MSG).

Just as the three Hebrew boys withstood the orders of the King and were not burned, scared, or singed, so shall it be for you. God is walking with you through every spiritual terrain and every bumpy road that seems so impossible to conquer. The effects of your ordeal will not leave you as though you have been in a fight, scared, bruised, or bloody.

"When you pass through the waters, I will be with you, and through the rivers, they will not overwhelm you. When you walk through the fire, you will not be burned or scorched, nor will the flame kindle upon you. "For I am the Lord your God, the Holy One of Israel, your Savior" (Isaiah 43:2-3AMP).

Move forward, understanding that suffering, pain, and troubles are not necessarily attacks from the enemy, but can be God's way of bringing you to a place of surety in Him. Know this: If God has brought you this far through the turbulences of life, He will continue keeping you. However, some tests are designed by Satan, and every one of those tests come to ultimately kill you, defeat you, and cause life to be unbearable.

You may not realize that everything we experience will work toward our good and for the glory of God. *"And we know that all things work together for good to them that love God, to them who are the called according to his purpose"(Romans 8:28 KJV).*

We will benefit from the sufferings. One of the purposes of suffering is to make us a stronger nation of people, and to become more Christ-like. You will learn that once a particular battle is over, and you look back, you will see that on the other side of the battle, you do have the victory.

You may never know what God will require you to go through to get you to a place of wholeness. Suffering for the sake of gaining something great will cost. There is a price that will be paid by you in order for you to walk and live a rich and fulfilled life.

Peter next uses the term "strengthen." The Greek definition of "strengthen" means "to confirm in spiritual knowledge and power; bodily vigor." The dictionary defines "strengthen" as "the state or quality of being strong; force; durability; the power to resist attack." Peter uses these words after he tells us about the attacks that will come from the enemy.

Chapter 12: Completely Whole I'm Willing to Endure

"Keep a cool head. Stay alert. The Devil is poised to pounce, and would like nothing better than to catch you napping. Keep your guard up. You're not the only ones plunged into these hard times. It's the same with Christians all over the world. So keep a firm grip on the faith. The suffering won't last forever. It won't be long before this generous God who has great plans for us in Christ—eternal and glorious plans they are!—will have you put together and on your feet for good. He gets the last word; yes, he does" (I Peter 5:8 MSG).

While under attack, you must stay on guard, stay alert, and do not be surprised by any of the attacks that come from Satan. Many times in the suffering, we have a tendency to weaken in our faith because we are so focused on the sufferings and what others have or have not done. Peter encourages us to be strong and firm while possessing spiritual knowledge and power. We have the ability to resist all the pressure, demands, and anxieties that may accompany the situation at the current moment. The battle goes on in the mind. If your mind thinks you can't make it, then you won't. Your mind will play tricks on you. One must take control of the thoughts in the mind that come to bring discouragement.

Prayer

Father, I come in the mighty name of Jesus, with a heart of thanksgiving for all You have done. I realize that You have equipped me for every battle I must face. I know You are carrying me and walking with me while I run this race. You have not called me to lose any fight; therefore, I have already defeated the enemy. I stand strong in You, and in the power of Your might. I will endure this, and every test I go through, knowing that You are with me.

Your Word declares that You are Emmanuel, God with us. Thank You that I can rely on You for everything I need while going through. The final outcome of my enduring is so I can experience wholeness. Thank You for not letting me go through this alone. You're a faithful God, and I will trust You as long as I live.

Today's confession: I will endure every test—for You are with me.

CHAPTER 13
Lord, I Have Not Lacked Anything

You are my Righteousness
Jehovah Tsidkenu (Jer 23:5, 6)

You are my Rewarder
Jehovah El Gmolah (Job 19:25)

You are my Provider
Jehovah Jireh (Gen 22:14)

You are my Protector
Jehovah Nissi (Ex 17:15, Ps 4:6)

You are my Peace
Jehovah Shalom (Judges 6:24, Deut 27:6)

You are my Shepherd
Jehovah Rohi (Gen 23)

You Fight for Me
Jehovah Sabbaoth (Is 1:24, Ps 46:7)

You are my Breakthrough
Jehovah Perazim (Micah 2:12-13, Is 10:27)

You are my Healer
Jehovah Rophe (Ex 15:22-26, Is 61:1)

You are Everywhere
Jehovah Shamma (Ex 48:35)

You are my Sanctifier
Jehovah M'Kaddesh (Lev 20:8)

Prayer

Dear Heavenly Father, I thank You. For You are my Healer, my Peace, the One who rewards me; my Righteousness, my Breakthrough, my Sanctifier, my Protector, my Shepherd, and God all by Yourself. There is no One besides You. Thank You for being everything I need. My life is complete and made whole by Your finished work on Calvary. I'm grateful this day that all my needs are met. I'm full, complete and satisfied because of You. Thank You, Jesus, that I'm living **Completely Whole.**

> "When you go, you will come to a secure people and a large land. For God has given it into your hands, a place where there is no lack of anything that is on the earth" (*Judges 18:10 KJV*)

ABOUT THE AUTHOR

Paulette Harper Johnson is a sought-after, keynote speaker for colleges, churches, and community groups. Every speech she delivers is motivating, and relevant to the challenges and issues faced by your audience. As an inspirational speaker, her desire is to empower, equip and transform the lives of women through her preaching and teaching from the Word of God. As a licensed and ordained minister, Paulette's passion is to minister the Word of God with boldness and accuracy so those who are dealing with life's complexities will become whole and walk in their God-given potential.

A woman of destiny, Paulette has accepted the call from God, and established herself as a best-selling, award-winning author. Paulette's writing career began in 2007 with her first published book; "That Was Then, This Is Now" which achieved national recognition by being awarded a finalist in the 2009 Next Generation Indie Book Award, and ranked consecutively on the Black Christian Publishers Bestsellers List for Independent Publishers, Non-Fiction. Published articles have appeared on CBN, Internet Café, WOW Magazine, Black Pearl Magazine and Divine Inspirations.

"Victorious Living for Women" (an anthology) is her second book, which features 40 incredible women who share stories of their life experiences, from their heart to yours. Collectively, these women have endured personal tragedies and have emerged empowered, encouraged, and victorious.

Paulette is the visionary behind "Write Now" (releasing the Word in you) literary workshops, which is designed to coach aspiring writers in the areas of creativity, development, and publication of Christian books. God has given her a desire for writers, especially those who want to write for the Lord. Through these workshops, it is her desire to provide information that will help aspiring authors' dreams come to reality, by providing tools, resources, and opportunities to help them succeed.

As a Certified Life Coach, Paulette's mission is to inspire you to define your purpose, and passion so you can discover your full potential for living your best life now. She specializes in seminars and workshops that are interactive, informative, and motivating.

She is blessed to be covered by her husband and pastor, Tony E. Johnson.

Paulette is available to speak, train, and facilitate at your upcoming event or conference.

To schedule Paulette Harper Johnson for a book club meeting, interview, book signing, speaking engagement, workshop, seminar, or other appearance, please contact her at: info@pauletteharper.com or visit her @ www.pauletteharper.com.

VICTORIOUS LIVING FOR WOMEN

ANTHOLOGY

ISBN-13: 978-0-9841815-0-6
ISBN-10: 0-9841815-0-4

Victorious Living for Women is filled with the inspiration, wisdom, and pathways to victory of 40 incredible women who share stories of their life experience, from their heart to yours. They have endured personal pain and have come through it empowered, encouraged, and victorious. As they take you on their personal journeys, you will find inspiration, encouragement, and blueprints for victory embedded in each chapter. You will discover principles for transforming your life. You can learn how to overcome fear, find you purpose, define your destiny, recover from divorce, and heal your heart. It will also help you with physical healing, dealing with the loss of loved ones, and so much more. This stellar assembly of women with inspiring true-life stories will captivate you throughout each page as you read how their lives were transformed from anger to joy, disappointment to destiny, and trial to victory. Their candor, wisdom, and inspiration can help you to pursue your path of becoming a victorious woman.

SuberPullins Publishing

Purchase copies at: www.pauletteharper.com

THAT WAS THEN, THIS IS NOW
THIS BROKEN VESSEL RESTORED

2009 Next Generation Indie Book Award Finalist
Black Christian News, Independent Publishers
Bestsellers List

ISBN-13: 978-1-60462-554-7
ISBN-10: 1-60462-554-6

How could God have a purpose for me amidst this mess? Why do such bad things happen to good people? If you've recently asked yourself these questions, Paulette Harper's *That was Then, This is Now* has the answers. Struggling to recover from a broken marriage and disappointed dreams, Paulette Harper gropes for meaning and understanding, and through her searching, God reveals Himself to her in ways she never before imagined possible. By sharing her struggles with transparency, she illustrates how a heart attitude of surrender allows God to use a broken vessel for His ultimate plans of glory.

Tate Publishing and Enterprises

Purchase copies at: www.pauletteharper.com

Made in the USA
Charleston, SC
04 January 2012